P9-CMT-001

A PATTERN FOR LIFE

Books by Archibald M. Hunter
Published by The Westminster Press

A Pattern for Life (Revised Edition)
Teaching and Preaching the New Testament
Paul and His Predecessors
Interpreting the Parables
Introducing the New Testament
Introducing New Testament Theology
Interpreting Paul's Gospel
Interpreting the New Testament, 1900–1950
The Work and Words of Jesus
The Message of the New Testament

William J Fay

A PATTERN
FOR LIFE

(Revised Edition)

*An Exposition
of the Sermon on the Mount,
Its Making, Its Exegesis and Its Meaning*

by
ARCHIBALD M. HUNTER

THE WESTMINSTER PRESS

Philadelphia

First Published in Great Britain in 1953
by SCM Press Ltd, under the title *Design for Life*
Revised edition, 1965

Library of Congress Catalog Card No. 66-11517

Eighth printing, 1976

Published by The Westminster Press®
Philadelphia, Pennsylvania

PRINTED IN THE UNITED STATES OF AMERICA

CONTENTS

Part One

THE MAKING, MANNER AND MATTER OF THE SERMON

Introduction		9
I	The Making of the Sermon	11
II	The Manner of the Sermon	18
III	The Matter of the Sermon	24

Part Two

THE EXEGESIS OF THE SERMON

Design for Life in the Kingdom of God	33

Part Three

THE MEANING OF THE SERMON

IV	The Sermon and its Interpreters	99
V	The Sermon and the Gospel	107
VI	The Sermon and the Ethic of Jesus	112
	Indexes	123

PREFACE

SINCE this book first appeared in 1953, several noted
scholars—e.g. Joachim Jeremias and W. D. Davies—have
illumined our understanding of the Sermon on the Mount,
and a modern martyr, Dietrich Bonhoeffer, has had great
influence through his classic of spiritual devotion based on
it. To take some account of their contributions, I have expanded chapter 1 ('The Making of the Sermon') and rewritten
Chapter IV ('The Sermon and Its Interpreters'). In the
middle portion of the book—the verse-by-verse exposition
—I have tried to improve or clarify the exegesis at various
points.

My general view of the Sermon—that it is Christ's design
for living for the men of the Kingdom and so, today, the
moral ideal for committed Christians—remains unchanged.
But I like Jeremias's way of putting things. What we have
in the words of the Sermon (he says) are really illustrations
of 'lived faith' (*gelebte Glaube*)—the suggested response-in-
life to the grace of God who brings the Kingdom in Christ.
And such faith, as Bonhoeffer reminds us, means above all
else obedience—or the grace becomes cheap grace.

King's College,   A. M. HUNTER
Aberdeen University,
December 1964

Part One

THE MAKING, MANNER AND MATTER OF THE SERMON

INTRODUCTION

AFTER nineteen hundred years the Sermon on the Mount still haunts men. They may praise it, as Mahatma Gandhi did; or like Nietzsche, they may curse it. They cannot ignore it. Its words are winged words, quick and powerful to rebuke, to challenge, to inspire. And though some turn from it in despair, it continues, like some mighty magnetic mountain, to attract to itself the greatest spirits of our race (many not Christians), so that if some world-wide vote were taken, there is little doubt that men would account it 'the most searching and powerful utterance we possess on what concerns the moral life'.

Sometimes in Christian history it has seemed as if men had almost forgotten it, or, perhaps deliberately, had tried to put it into cold storage. But always it has leapt to life again, to serve as inspiration and challenge. And whenever human society falls on evil days, and moral decay sets in (as in Tolstoy's Russia), men return to it wistfully, half-persuaded that in its hundred-odd verses is the cure for human ills. Sometimes men talk as if the Sermon were all 'plain sailing', as simple as the Highway Code: a collection of plain and practical rules for living which must commend themselves to all right-thinking men. They cry out that all we need to do is to put these principles of Jesus into the statute books of the nations, and all will be well. It is then that others arise to ask, Is the Sermon indeed all plain sailing? And is it a morality for all men? So the debate goes on. Some take the Sermon as a sort of canon within the canon—assure us that the whole essence of the Gospel is to be found in it—and bid us discard the framework of miracle and Messianism in which it has been embedded. Others, taught their Christianity at Pauline or Reformation sources, are just as sure that not here lies the heart of the Gospel. The Sermon (they say) serves to show us how much we stand in need of salvation: it is a great indictment of that human sin which the Gospel of God's grace in the Cross is designed to meet and cure.

What is the truth about the Sermon? Was it delivered as it stands? To whom? The Church or the world? In what sense is it original? What was its place in early Christianity? Did Jesus design it as a new law to be as binding on the new Israel as the Torah had been on the old? And what is the Sermon's relevance and importance for us today who live in other times, under other skies, and are vexed by other problems? These are some of the questions we shall try to handle in this book.

I

THE MAKING OF
THE SERMON

T H E Sermon on the Mount is to be found in the fifth, sixth
and seventh chapters of the Gospel according to St
Matthew. It is the first of five great discourses characteristic of Matthew who introduces it with these words:

And seeing the multitudes, he went up into the mountain
[perhaps better the 'hill-country']: and when he had sat down,
his disciples came unto him: and he opened his mouth and
taught them saying.

The ordinary church member, hearing these words read
in church, naturally enough supposes that Jesus delivered
the substance of the following three chapters to his disciples on some Galilean hill-side in one non-stop discourse,
and that one of the disciples (probably Matthew, a man of
some education) with gifts as a reporter preserved notes of
it which were later incorporated in the first Gospel. The
truth is not quite so simple. We need not doubt that Jesus
did give this teaching to his disciples in some such setting;
but it is tolerably certain that he did not give them all this
teaching in a single sermon. (If he had done so, only those
disciples with Macaulay-esque memories could have
remembered it all.) Beyond doubt the Sermon gathers together sayings of our Lord uttered on many different
occasions. It is 'a mosaic of the more striking fragments of
perhaps twenty discourses'.

A knowledge of Jewish ways of teaching will help us to

understand how these fragments first took shape. Our Lord was commonly addressed as 'rabbi'; and though, by the then current standards, he was a very unorthodox one, it is a reasonable inference that his teaching technique resembled that of other rabbis. Now we know how these rabbis taught. First, the rabbi would discourse to his disciples on some topic; then the results of the discourse would be summed up in certain easily remembered propositions. A. C. Deane[1] has described the method very clearly:

The method of the Jewish religious teachers was to compress into a few succinct and pointed sentences the expression of any truth they deemed of special importance. Then the teacher would repeat the sentences many times with his disciples, until they knew them by heart. There is every reason to suppose that Jesus used this accustomed method of teaching by repetition. The pointed gnomic sentences of which the Sermon on the Mount consists are exactly suited to this purpose.

Thus we may suppose the Sermon to have originated; and indeed within the Sermon itself we can trace what look like two 'sermonettes' of Jesus, each no doubt delivered on a specific occasion, though the Evangelist has added to them other sayings of Jesus. One is Matt. 5.21-48, the discourse on the Old Law and the New with its six antitheses. The other is a short sermon on true worship treating of three topics: almsgiving, prayer and fasting (Matt. 6.1-6; 16-18).

This however was only the Galilean beginning of things. Two questions now arise: (1) Can we be sure that these sayings of Jesus have been faithfully transmitted by the first Christians? (2) How came they to be gathered together in the masterly order in which we now have them in Matthew's Gospel?

In the earliest years of the Church the sayings of Jesus were transmitted orally. Oral tradition of course always

[1] *How to understand the Gospels*, 71.

involves the risk of distortion in transmission. Yet there are sound reasons for believing that our Lord's sayings escaped serious corruption in the process. To begin with, the first Christians were Jews, and we know from rabbinical sources that the Jewish community took pains to transmit its oral tradition, e.g. the sayings of the great rabbis, faithfully. Next, the references to 'tradition' in the New Testament, especially in Paul's letters, show that the early Christians had a like concern for trustworthy transmission of Gospel truth. Finally, as already suggested, this process of careful transmission began with Jesus himself who as a teacher made his disciples repeat and learn by heart what he taught them. We may therefore feel considerable confidence that the sayings of Jesus collected in the Sermon on the Mount are substantially authentic.[2]

To answer the second question we must say a little about the origin of Matthew's Gospel.

According to most modern scholars this Gospel was written in Syrian Antioch AD 80-85. It came to be linked with the apostle Matthew, possibly because he made a collection of Jesus' sayings used in its composition. The name of the actual author eludes us, but a study of his book reveals him for the man he was—a Greek-speaking Jewish Christian with something of the Law still clinging to him—or, to borrow words from his Gospel, 'a scribe discipled to the kingdom of heaven'. He wrote his book for Jewish Christians, as he wished to portray Jesus as the promised Messiah.

When he sat down to write, 'Matthew' (as we may conveniently call him) had three sources of material at his disposal: (i) Mark's Gospel written about AD 65 in Rome; (ii) a collection of Jesus' sayings made about AD 50 (used also by Luke) and now known among scholars as 'Q' (German, *Quelle* 'source'); and (iii) Gospel tradition of his

[2] See H. Riesenfeld, *The Gospel Tradition and Its Beginnings* (1959).

own—both sayings of Jesus and stories about him—which may be denominated 'M'.

If now, narrowing our enquiry, we ask how Matthew came to produce the magnificent compend of Jesus' moral teaching (which since Augustine has been called 'the Sermon on the Mount') we must consider the other 'Sermon' found in the Gospels—that recorded in Luke 6.20-49 and commonly called the 'Sermon on the Plain' (Luke 6.17).

Matthew's Sermon, which comprises 107 verses, starts with Beatitudes and ends with the parable of the Two Builders. Luke's Sermon, which has only 30 verses, also begins with Beatitudes and ends with the same parable. Moreover, all but 6 verses of Luke's Sermon have parallels more or less close in the Sermon on the Mount. How are we to explain the connexion between the two Sermons?

Thus: both the M and the Q sources contained Sermons which overlapped at certain points. (Both began with Beatitudes, both had sayings about love of enemies, and both ended with the building parable.) Probably Luke's Sermon represented the Sermon as it stood in Q. Matthew, having before him both M and Q, used the M Sermon as his framework and fitted into it sayings from the Q Sermon, adding also other sayings of Jesus to be paralleled elsewhere in Luke's Gospel (e.g. Luke 12.22-34).

Of the Sermon on the Mount's 107 verses, about 40 probably came from Q: Matthew drew the rest from M.

Let us end this chapter on Matthew's finished Sermon with some general observations.

First: From the manner in which he has marshalled Jesus' teaching in his Sermon, we may surmise that he had the needs of catechumens in view. To the first disciples who had followed Jesus and entered the Kingdom of God, Jesus had sought to show how God meant the men of the Kingdom how to live. What more natural and right than that later church leaders, wishing to show their converts the moral ideal to which their Lord called them, should gather together the teaching of Jesus as Matthew has done, to serve as summary and design for life in the Kingdom of God?

Second: Matthew's Gospel contains five great discourses of Jesus, the first of which is said to have been given on 'a mountain'. Not surprisingly some scholars, remembering Moses, Mount Sinai, and the five books of the Pentateuch, have suggested that Matthew deliberately set out to depict Jesus as the new Moses delivering a new Law (or *Torah*) on a new Sinai.

The suggestion fails to convince, for several reasons: (a) If this was Matthew's purpose, he made a poor job of executing it; for no clear parallelism with the Pentateuch is traceable in his Gospel, neither are Exodus motifs very plentiful; (b) What Matthew really intended was to portray a Jesus who was Messiah both in *word* and in *deed*. This is why he follows up the three chapters of the Sermon (5-7) with two chapters (8-9) recording no less than ten miracles of Jesus. (c) In the Sermon 'Mosaic categories are transcended': if the Pentateuch shows us Moses commanding as *mediator*, the Sermon shows us Jesus commanding as *Lord*. For Matthew, Someone greater than Moses is here.

Third: Nonetheless, it is quite clear that Matthew wishes his readers to find in the Sermon the new moral law of the Messiah. This impression plus the strong stress in the Sermon upon doing the commandments of Jesus—all suggesting a religion of 'works', of achievement—have led many to think that Matthew is at sharp variance with Paul on the whole issue of law and grace.

That this impression is basically wrong, deeper study will show.

Consider first Christianity according to Matthew. Judge it merely by the Sermon on the Mount, i.e. in isolation from the rest of his Gospel, and you may easily conclude that he believes in justification by 'law works'. But this is but another example of the danger of taking things out of their proper contexts. Later in this book we shall show that the ethic of the Sermon is essentially one of grace because the *prius* and presupposition of every saying in it is the Good News of the advent of God's New Order of grace—the Kingdom of God. Seen in this light, the precepts of the Sermon become illustrations and examples of the new quality of life which is the proper response to the experienced grace of God in Christ. And even if we confine ourselves to the Sermon as it stands now in Matthew, the Beatitudes which begin it and the parable about doing Christ's words at its end, show the Sermon to be spanned by the great arch of grace and law.

It was not essentially different with Paul's Christianity. Sometimes, reading him, we get the impression that for him the Christian life is simply the reaction of gratitude to God's forgiving grace in Christ—a life of complete freedom unfettered or even unguided by any rule, pattern or law. But this is far from the whole truth. Percipient modern scholars have noted that much in Paul's letters suggests that for him 'conformity to Christ, his teaching and life, took the place for Paul of conformity to the Jewish Torah' —that in fact he found in Jesus' words and deeds a new Torah. Certainly Paul regarded the precepts of Jesus as forming an authoritative pattern for Christian living which he called 'the law of Christ' (Gal. 6.2; I Cor. 9.21. Cf; Rom. 10.6ff.) Thus grace and law—'the law of Christ'—spanned the arch of Paul's Christianity also; and if Paul's eyes had ever fallen on Matthew's Sermon we doubt if he would have found much in it incompatible with his understanding of the Gospel.

The truth is that this arch of grace and law ultimately goes back to One whom both Matthew and Paul acknowledged as Lord and Master. In the message of Jesus we find both offer (grace) and moral demand (law). The Jesus of history was both Saviour from sin and Teacher of righteousness; and in the great invitation he addressed to all labouring under the burdens of Jewish legalism (Matt. 11.28-30) we find both succour and demand, both grace and law.[3]

[3] See W. D. Davies, *The Setting of the Sermon on the Mount,* Chapters V-VII.

II

THE MANNER OF

THE SERMON

I

T H E manner of the Sermon is, first of all, *poetical*. If we printed it in our Bibles as it should be printed, we should have to deal in couplets and even stanzas. For much of the Sermon is Hebrew poetry—Hebrew poetry as it had been written centuries before by prophet, sage and psalmist. Nearly forty years ago C. F. Burney of Oxford worked all this out in his book *The Poetry of our Lord*. We need not go into all his technicalities; the main point is that, even in an English dress, we can detect in the Sermon not only that 'parallelism' which is the chief formal feature of Semitic poetry but also clearly marked rhythm.

'Parallelism' is 'a rhyming of thoughts': the correspondence in sense of one line with another. Anyone can recognize it in such familiar lines as these:

> The heavens declare the glory of God;
> And the firmament sheweth his handiwork.
>
> (Ps. 19.1)

or in this excerpt from the book of Proverbs:

> A wise son maketh a glad father;
> But a foolish son is the heaviness of his mother.
>
> (Prov. 10.1)

In the former example, the second line echoes and reinforces the thought of the first in different words. In the latter, the second line states the precisely opposite truth. The experts style the first kind of parallelism 'synonymous', the second 'antithetic'; but they distinguish other sorts which they call 'synthetic' and 'climatic'. These refinements need not concern us here.

Now, similar poetic forms occur in the Sermon on the Mount. Thus,

> Give not that which is holy unto the dogs,
> Neither cast your pearls before the swine.
>
> (Matt. 7.6)

is a sample of 'synonymous' parallelism. Matt. 7.17 is 'antithetic':

> Every good tree bringeth forth good fruit,
> But the corrupt tree bringeth forth evil fruit.

But parallelism can be a matter not only of couplets like these but even of strophes, as in our Lord's words about prayer:

> Ask, and it shall be given you;
> Seek, and ye shall find;
> Knock, and it shall be opened unto you.
>
> For every one that asketh receiveth,
> And he that seeketh findeth,
> And to him that knocketh it shall be opened.
>
> (Matt. 7.7f.)

Rhythm, the other main feature of Semitic poetry, is also found in the Sermon. (Here, by 'rhythm' we mean not some regular system of metre depending on feet each of so many syllables but a system of so many rhythmical beats—sometimes four, oftener three, and sometimes two—in each line, with sometimes a pause in the middle, a caesura.) The best example is perhaps the Lord's Prayer in Matthew's version which, marking the beats, we will print as Burney does:

Our Fáther in heáven	hállowed by thy náme,
Thy kíngdom cóme;	Thy wíll be dóne;
As in the héavens,	só on eárth.
Our dáily breád	gíve us to-dáy;
And forgíve us our débts,	as we forgíve our débtors;
And leád us not into temptátion,	but delíver us from évil.

Printed thus, the poetical symmetry is unmistakable. We have two stanzas, each of three lines, and each of the three lines has four beats. Anyone can see how such poetic form would conduce to easy memorizing. Are we to say that all this is merely accidental? Is it not rather the work of One who so framed his pattern Prayer that he might fix it surely in the memory of his disciples?

II

Chesterton once advised a young friend:

> And don't believe in anything
> That can't be told in coloured pictures.

One of the secrets of the perennial freshness of the great Sermon is that it is radically *pictorial*. Not only does it employ parables, but it abounds in vivid, concrete speech and is illustrated direct from common life and nature.

We see the germ of the parable in such sayings as 'A city that is set on an hill cannot be hid' or 'The eye is the lamp of the body'. In its simplest form the parable is a figurative saying, whether it be a metaphor or a simile. We get what we normally reckon a parable when this is expanded into a picture like that of the Splinter and the Plank (what a picture it is too! A man with a plank in his eye!), or into a story like that of the Defendant or that of the Two Houses. But the Sermon does not contain many parables proper, for Matthew kept the chief ones for later discourses (e.g. chap. 13).

Fitzgerald once posed the question, What would have

become of Christianity if Jeremy Bentham had had the writing of the parables? We need not pursue the enquiry. What Fitzgerald had in mind was the intensely concrete and visualizing character of our Lord's style. We Occidentals moralize in abstract terms; Jesus deals in 'things which you can touch and see'. When we should say, 'Charity should never be obtrusive', he says, 'When you give alms, sound not a trumpet before you'. If we had to express the thought in Matt. 7.6, we should probably say, 'Exercise reserve in your communication of religious truth'. Jesus says, 'Give not that which is holy unto the dogs'. We talk of Providence; but Jesus abjures long abstract words like this. What he says is: 'Your heavenly Father knows that you have need of all these things. . . . If you then being evil know how to give good gifts to your children, how much more will your Father who is in heaven give good things to those who ask him?'

Akin to all this is the way the Sermon keeps close to human life and everyday reality for its illustrations. Think of the variety of 'characters' who make their brief entrances in the sayings of the Sermon, conjured up for us sometimes by a single word. They range through all grades of society from 'Solomon in all his glory' to the beggar by the roadside (5.42). We catch a glimpse of the Roman official 'conscripting' one of the subject race to carry his baggage for a mile (5.41); the judge in the law-court with the 'constable' waiting to clap the guilty man in gaol (5.25f.); the religious 'humbug' at the street-corner parading his piety with a face rapidly disappearing under a veneer of holy dirt (6.5, 16); the local builder beginning a new house and casting about carefully for a bit of solid rock to serve as foundation (7.24); the house-breaker ready with his trowel to 'dig through' a clay wall on a dark night (6.19). All these and many more serve to 'illustrate' the Sermon: the village women heating their ovens with 'the lilies of the fields' (6.30); their children clamouring

for a piece of bread or a bit of fish (7.9f.); these, with all
the sights and sounds of nature: sun and rain, wind and
flood, thistle and thorn, vine and fig, with birds and moths,
dogs and swine, sheep and wolves. For the 'divineness of
the natural order' is a major premise of our Lord's teaching; and since nature and super-nature are one order for
him, he can see in these things a revelation of God and his
ways, and use them in the service of his heavenly truth.

III

The third feature of the Sermon's style worth noting is
its *proverbial* nature.

Having said this, we should perhaps add a word of warning about proverbs. It is of the very nature of proverbial
teaching that, while it is easy to remember and general in
form, it states truth in a vivid, extreme, hyperbolical way.
Proverbs indeed are principles stated in extremes, without
modification, often requiring to be balanced by their seem-
ing contraries. Since they often deal in sharply-phrased
paradox—the paradox being meant to stimulate and stab
us broad awake—we must, if we are to avoid the peril of
a crude literalism in interpretation, always be seeking for
the principle that underlies the proverb, the truth behind
the paradox, ceaselessly resisting the temptation to water
it down into a moral commonplace.

Take for instance our Lord's sayings in the Sermon about
'plucking out the eye' and 'cutting off the hand' (Matt.
5.29-30). Interpret them with rigorous literalism, and we
may end up, as Origen did, by mutilating ourselves. We
may then ask ourselves how far our action has advanced
us in our Christian discipleship. If we cut off the hand
that pilfers, do we kill the temptation to steal? If we
pluck out the offending eye, do we mortify the passion of
lust? Common-sense ought to tell us that it is the principle,
not the literal meaning, which matters here—the principle
of rigorous self-discipline in the service of the Kingdom

of God. Paul took Christ's meaning, whether he knew this saying or not, when he wrote to the Corinthians: 'I maul and master my body, in case, after preaching to other people, I am disqualified myself.' (I Cor. 9.27. Moffatt.)

Here, while we are talking of proverbs and principles, we may usefully add a note on the moral imperatives which we find in the Sermon (especially in Matt. 5.21-48). Their interpretation has puzzled many; but light comes if we distinguish between *mandata* and *exempla*. *Mandata* are moral imperatives stating deep, broad principles; *exempla* are illustrations of these principles in action. Thus 'resist not evil' (or 'resist not him that is evil' [Matt. 5.39]) is an imperative stating a principle: the principle of non-vindictiveness in personal relations, not of non-resistance to evil in any and every circumstance. Then follow in the Sermon four vivid illustrations of the principle: 'turn the other cheek', 'let your opponent have your cloak', etc. To take these illustrations quite literally and erect them into principles of action is to land oneself in absurdity. Similarly when Jesus says 'swear not at all' (Matt. 5.34), he is calling for absolute sincerity in speech, not prohibiting oaths in all circumstances (e.g. in the law-court). And, finally, when he adjures his disciples 'not to lay up treasures on earth' (Matt. 6.19) he is not prohibiting all thrift and condemning the banking system out of hand, but warning them gravely against the dangers of devotion to what has been called 'the metallic trinity'.

III

THE MATTER OF
THE SERMON

IN this chapter the question before us is, In what sense is the matter of the Sermon original?

So long ago as the second century Celsus stoutly maintained that Christ had raided the wise men of Greece for his wisdom. Our Lord's saying about the camel and the needle's eye was but a poor plagiarized version of Plato's that it is hard to find a man who is both rich and good. From that day till our own, critics of Christianity have pounced with joy on any saying in pagan philosopher or Oriental sage which, by echoing or anticipating some portion of Christ's teaching, seemed to impair the Christian conception of him as the Lord of all good life. 'Where is the originality of Matt. 5.44f.', they have said, 'when you can find a pagan like Seneca declaring, "If you would imitate God, be gracious to the ungracious; for the sun shines on the wicked, and the sea is open to pirates".' Or they have pointed out that, six centuries before Christ, the Chinese sage, Lao Tsze, was saying, 'He that humbleth himself shall be preserved entire. He that has little shall succeed. He that hath much shall go astray.' About all, in our own times, apologists for Judaism have laboured to gather rabbinical parallels to this or that saying of our Lord. We have been told that every single petition in the Lord's Prayer can be found somewhere in the Jewish liturgies or the sayings of the Jewish Fathers, and that both Tobit and Hillel taught the Golden Rule as well as Christ. And so on.

Confronted by such parallels, how can we Christians seriously maintain that the teaching of the Sermon on the Mount is original?

Before we attempt a reply, we had better ask the question, What precisely is meant by originality in a case like this? When we claim that Christ's teaching is original, do we mean that no one had ever said anything like it before? By originality do we mean utter newness?

If this were the case we had to defend, we would be wise to throw in our brief at once. It is futile to claim that there were no anticipations of the moral truth which Christ taught. To be sure, there are passages in the Sermon on the Mount which fair-minded Jews like C. G. Monte- fiore allow to transcend in their moral grandeur anything said by the rabbis, e.g. Matt. 5.38-48. But in a problem of this kind originality is not a matter of utter newness but rather the power of seeing old things in a new light. We need to remember that the originality of a moral teacher cannot be like that of an inventor or explorer who forfeits his claim as soon as it is shown that another has forestalled him in the field. A claim to originality of this kind in the field of theology or ethics rightly awakens our suspicions. 'Really great moral teachers,' says C. S. Lewis, 'never do produce new moralities. It is quacks and cranks who do that.'[1]

The great moral teacher is better compared with the artist or the writer. The work of the great artist is not to manufacture new paints but with old ones to produce great pictures. The work of the great writer is not to flood the language with 'neologisms' but to set old and familiar words to new and glorious uses. And here we may usefully cite Shakespeare, by common consent the most creative and original writer in our language. What do we mean when we call him original? Do we mean that he owes no debt to the past? We have no sooner made the suggestion than we

[1] *Christian Behaviour*, 16.

know it to be false. In every play he borrowed from the past. He took his plots and characters from many sources —from Plutarch, Holinshed and many another. Yet Shakespeare is original—and original because, though he borrowed both word and idea, all was passed through the alembic of that sovereign mind and transformed by his genius.

The analogy is inadequate. Jesus is not for us an ethical Shakespeare; he is much more. Yet it does help us to define originality in the matter before us. It is not a case of wiping the slate clean and beginning *de novo*, as though all that had been said and thought by man about God and man and good and evil had been false and futile. It is rather the power to take the old truth, to transform it, to perfect it: to turn the lead into gold, the carbon into diamond, and in so doing to discard much that was accidental, transient and for a day.

If then we find that this or that element in Christ's teaching has a partial parallel in Plato or Seneca, Hillel or Lao Tsze, we need not be disturbed or shocked. Let us remember in particular that Christ served himself heir to the great religious heritage of Israel, and that he 'came not to destroy but to fulfil'. It would be strange therefore if we did not find in that heritage anticipations of the moral truth so wonderfully set before us in the Sermon on the Mount. But there is another, and no less important, consideration. If truth is eternal and God is one, we should not think it strange that others should have uttered moral truths which anticipate Christ. To discover such parallels is to remind ourselves that God has not left himself without a witness outside the orbit of the Christian revelation.

Christ's work [says Votaw] was not to make a clean sweep of all existing religious conceptions and phraseology as though the world had never had any vision of God, or truth, or goodness, or right; on the contrary, he came to show that the Old Testament revelation was, in its best thought and teaching, a true divine revelation which he would exalt and perfect. Jesus was not original in the sense that he created a wholly new fabric of religious ideas, or introduced a wholly new set of religious terms; that kind of originality was made impossible by the fact that God was already in his world. Jesus' originality —and the term is not misapplied—consisted in his ability to separate the true from the false, the permanent from the transient, the perfect from the imperfect; and then to carry forward the whole circle of ideas and practices to their ideal expression.[2]

It is along these lines that we must seek the originality of Jesus as a moral teacher. Three things in the Sermon seem to us to set it in a place by itself in the long history of man's thinking about the good life: its insight into essential morality, its inwardness, and its universality.

William Sanday[3] once described the teaching of Jesus as 'the distilled essence of the Old Testament'. The Sermon exemplifies the truth of the phrase. All the accidentals and irrelevancies—the mass of ceremonial details in the Law— he ignores, throwing all stress on the *moral* elements. Elsewhere in the Gospels Jesus takes the commandment, 'Thou shalt love thy neighbour as thyself', out of a mass of ritual rubbish. But he goes further. He sums up the whole Law in the twin-command of love to God and love to one's fellow-man. So it is also when we contrast Christ's teaching with that of the rabbis. They have their flashes of moral insight, no doubt, but what a searching for them we have amid long dreary tracts of rabbinizing about the Law, and how refreshing it is to turn from the Talmud to the Sermon! 'All of Jesus' moral teaching,' say the Jewish scholars, 'is in the Talmud!' 'No doubt,' we may retort, 'and how much more?' Instead of piling up a multitude of precepts which can only perplex and befog the faithful, Jesus lays down a few deep principles. Instead of setting ritual and ethical on a dead level, so that it seems as sinful to eat certain foods

[2] *H.D.B.* Vol. V, 34.
[3] *Outlines of the Life of Christ,* 66.

or to carry a burden on the Sabbath as it is to commit murder or adultery, Jesus goes right to the heart of essential morality—to obedience to God out of a pure heart. It is th's unique and intense concentration on the moral, says Gerhard Kittel, which makes all the difference between the Teacher of the Sermon and the teachers of Judaism. 'The originality of Jesus,' Wellhausen declared, 'consists in this, that he had the feeling for what was true and eternal amid a chaotic mass of rubbish, and that he enunciated it with the greatest emphasis.' And that is why you will search Jewish—or for that matter, any other literature—for a document which for ethical purity and sublimity is fit to stand beside the Sermon.

A second mark of the Sermon's originality is its *inwardness*. It would be wrong to say that all Jewish teachers were ignorant that true righteousness has its home in the heart. The Psalmist's 'Behold, thou desirest truth in the inward parts' does not stand alone in the Old Testament; nor were the great rabbis unaware that the state of the heart is the paramount thing. But where shall we find a document, comparable to the Sermon, whose demand is so steady and insistent for 'a morality in the blood and in the bone'? Legal religion, like that of the scribes and Pharisees in our Lord's time, always attacks the problem of right and wrong conduct from the outside, and proceeds to lay down rules and regulations. Jesus tracks sin to its lair in the heart of man. The Law, he says, condemns murder: I condemn the hate in the heart. The Law condemns adultery: I condemn the passion of lust. The Law limits revenge to tit-for-tat. I condemn the vindictive spirit. In fine, Jesus *internalizes* morality.[4] Conduct, he says, is like the fruit of a tree. If you wish good fruit, first make the tree good. The important thing is not what a man does but what he is. And if it be true, as A. E. Taylor claims,[5]

[4] L. H. Marshall, *The Challenge of New Testament Ethics,* 70.
[5] *The Faith of a Moralist,* I, 224.

that Christianity stands above all other religions in its inwardness, it is due to him who first pronounced the beatitude of 'the pure in heart'.

Note finally the *universality* of the Sermon. It is purged clean of all exclusiveness and particularism. It deals with *das allgemeine menschliche*; it concerns itself not with the Jew as Jew but with man as man; it looks beyond Palestine to the whole world. The disciples are 'the salt of the earth', and their task is to be torch-bearers of the true light to the whole world. 'You shall be catholic,' Jesus tells them, 'as your heavenly Father is catholic'. As God's grace makes no distinctions between man and man, so they, as imitators of God, are to make none. The Lord's Prayer may have been in the beginning a pattern Prayer for a handful of Jews; but what amazes us in the Prayer—what makes it the Family Prayer of a world-wide Church—is its innocence of everything that is narrow and nationalistic, its sweep and range. In its brief compass lies the whole world of divine and human concerns. Or consider the Golden Rule. Here is a guide to the good life which any man may use. Difficult of performance it may be; but all men know in their hearts that it is but the cap-stone of a morality which commands the admiration of all who have pondered the problem of right living. C. E. M. Joad speaks for most when he says: 'We know, in fact, that we ought to live as Christ enjoined. We may say that Christ's prescription of good living is wholly impracticable or is much too difficult; but that does not alter our conviction that it is the right prescription.'[6]

[6] *Science and Ethics*, 28.

Part Two

THE EXEGESIS OF
THE SERMON

DESIGN FOR LIFE IN THE KINGDOM OF GOD
(Matt. 5-7)
A. THE LIFE DESCRIBED:
    (*a*) its characteristics (the Beatitudes)   5.3-12
    (*b*) its influence (salt and light)   13-16

B. ITS RELATION TO THE OLD ORDER   17-20

C. ITS OUTWORKINGS:
    (*a*) in thought, word and deed
        (six antitheses)   21-48
    (*b*) in worship (almsgiving, prayer and
        fasting)   6.1-18
    (*c*) in trust and devotion   19-34
    (*d*) in treatment of others   7.1-12

D. THE WAY OF LIFE
    profession and practice   13-27

DESIGN FOR LIFE
IN THE KINGDOM
OF GOD

A. THE LIFE DESCRIBED

(a) Its characteristics: The Beatitudes. 5.3-12. Q + M. Luke 6

3   Blessed are the poor in spirit: 6.20
      for theirs is the kingdom of heaven.

4   Blessed are they that mourn: 6.21b
      for they shall be comforted.

5   Blessed are the meek:
      for they shall inherit the earth.

6   Blessed are they that hunger and thirst   6.21a
        after righteousness:
      for they shall be filled.

7   Blessed are the merciful:
      for they shall obtain mercy.

8   Blessed are the pure in heart:
      for they shall see God.

9   Blessed are the peacemakers:
      for they shall be called sons of God.

10   Blessed are they that have been persecuted
        for righteousness' sake:
      for theirs is the kingdom of heaven.

11   Blessed are ye, when men shall reproach you,   6.22f.
      and persecute you, and say all manner of evil
      against you, falsely,[1] for my sake.

12   Rejoice and be exceeding glad:
      for so persecuted they the prophets
      which were before you.

The Beatitudes are the soul of the Sermon on the Mount.

[1] *Falsely*, omitted by some Western authorities, as by Luke, is probably a gloss.

'Blessed' means 'Ah, the happiness of', and beatitude is the happiness of the man who, in communion with God, lives the life that is life indeed. The Beatitudes of Jesus describe the character of the men who, living under God's Fatherly Rule made manifest in Jesus, enjoy that happiness even here and now, though its perfection belongs to the heavenly world.

They form a noble preface to the Sermon which will outline the moral ideal for the men of the Kingdom. Though in Matthew's version there are eight of them (Luke has only four, and these in the second person plural), we should think not so much of eight different types of character as of one ideal character seen from eight different angles—one diamond with eight facets. And the character which the Beatitudes depict is essentially that of Jesus himself. 'In the character of Jesus the distinctive beauties of the Beatitudes harmonize like the colours in a mosaic. He is poor in spirit, a mourner, meek and lowly in heart. He hungers for the supremacy of righteousness, is merciful, pure in heart, the Prince of peace, and suffers for righteousness' sake—yet none of these virtues is cultivated at the expense of another. They blend in his character in their true proportion and express the spirit of perfect love.'[2]

The end of each Beatitude tells us what Christ means by his promise of blessing. It can be comprehensively described as 'the Kingdom of heaven', which is Matthew's phrase for what the other evangelists call 'the Kingdom of God'. The kingdom is just another name for the salvation of which Jesus is the Bringer. What it means the various Beatitudes make clear: 'comforting', dominion, the vindication of God's cause, mercy on the Day of Judgment, the Beatific Vision, and the ineffable glory of divine sonship.

Two other features of the Beatitudes need to be underlined. The first is that they are *Messianic*: As we study them in detail, we shall see that again and again they recall

[2] Devine, *The Religion of the Beatitudes*, 9.

the Messianic promises of the Old Testament, and especially those in 'Second Isaiah', the evangelical prophet. To be sure, Jesus' own Messiahship is veiled—he does not in the Beatitudes expressly call himself the Messiah. But when he promises the Kingdom to the 'poor' or 'comforting' for the 'mourners', when he speaks of the 'meek' inheriting the earth or calls suffering for his sake blessed, the implication is (as surely as in his sermon in the Nazareth synagogue) that in himself and his ministry the ancient promises are being fulfilled.

The other thing to note is that, as Wilder says, the ethics of the Beatitudes 'are not so much ethics of obedience as *ethics of grace*'.[3] They imply God as a gracious giver and man as a humble receiver. They do not mean: you must do these things in order to deserve and win the divine approval. Rather do they say: God gives his blessedness to those who claim no merit for themselves but, knowing their own heart's need, are content to rest wholly on the mercy of God.

3 *The First Beatitude.*

Luke's version runs: 'Blessed are ye poor, for yours is the kingdom of God.' Who are 'the poor' of this Beatitude? Since there is nothing ethical, let alone blessed, in economic poverty as such, Matthew's addition 'in spirit' points the way to the right interpretation.* Again and again in the Psalms 'poor' and 'pious' are synonymous for those who out of their need cast themselves wholly on God for their salvation. They are 'the poor' of Isa. 61.1 to whom the Servant of the Lord is anointed to preach 'good tidings'. Cf. Luke 4.18. We are to think then not of 'the poor spirited' but of those who 'feel their spiritual need', who

[3] Amos Wilder, *Eschatology and Ethics in the New Testament*, 120.

* The phrase 'poor in spirit' has turned up in the Dead Sea Scrolls, so that Luke's 'poor' is not necessarily more original.

acknowledge their spiritual poverty, 'the beggars before God'. To such the kingdom is promised.

'We are all beggars,' said the dying Luther. The Gospel is not for the proud and the self-sufficient, but for those who, owning their sinfulness and insufficiency, cast themselves on the mercy of God in Christ.

4 *The Second Beatitude.*

Luke's version runs, 'Blessed are ye that weep now: for ye shall laugh'. Who are the mourners? Not primarily those who

> Sigh for the touch of a vanished hand
> And the sound of a voice that is still,

though these are not excluded. We find the clue in Isa. 61.2, 'to comfort all that mourn' and in the description of Simeon (Luke 2.25) who waited for 'the comforting of Israel'. The mourners are those 'to whom the evil that is in the world is a continual grief', those who mourn the apparent eclipse of God's people and cause, and long for a Saviour to arise upon the earth. (In Jesus' day 'the Comforter' was one of the Messiah's names, and the 'Comfort' prophecies of Isaiah, e.g. 40.1f.; 61.2f., were referred to the Messianic Age. See Ecclus 48.24, where Ben Sira says of Isaiah:

> By a special inspiration he saw the last things
> And comforted the mourners in Zion.)

They shall be comforted. These words contain a veiled claim to Messiahship. It is as if Jesus said, 'Yes, and I will be their comforter'. It is a promise in part fulfilled in the mighty acts of the Gospel Story—in the sacrifice of the Cross, the victory of the Resurrection, and the gift of the Spirit—a promise to be completely fulfilled when, at the consummation of all things, sin and death will be finally done away and 'God shall wipe away every tear from their eyes' (Rev. 7.17).

5 *The Third Beatitude.*

This has no counterpart in Luke.

For the modern man with only the AV before him no Beatitude is more perplexing than this one. In it Jesus seems to be promising the meek the mastery of the world, when in fact everybody knows that the weak—and the meek—go to the wall. But was this really Jesus' meaning?

Part of the trouble lies in the AV's translation of the Greek *praus* by 'meek'. 'Meek' has for us a pejorative meaning which it does not have in the Bible. When we read that 'the man Moses was very meek' or hear Jesus claim to be 'meek and lowly in heart', we think not of weakness but of the gentleness and humility that go with strength in the greatest. And 'gentle' is probably the best English equivalent we can find for the Greek, as the NEB suggests: 'How blest are those of a gentle spirit.'

But is Jesus really promising 'the gentle' world-dominion? In Ps. 37.11, where we find the same words, the meaning is, 'They shall inherit the (promised) land'. Now we know from passages like Isa. 57.13 and 60.21 that this phrase acquired a figurative and Messianic meaning. So it must be in this Beatitude: 'How blessed are the gentle ones! They shall have a share in Messiah's kingdom.'

We may compare I Peter 1.4 where language first used of the 'old Canaan' is applied to the Christians' heavenly inheritance.

6 *The Fourth Beatitude.*

Luke has: 'Blessed are ye that hunger now: for ye shall be filled.'

The chief question here is, What does Matthew mean by 'righteousness'? *Dikaiosune* is a very chameleon among New Testament words. Some take it here to mean simply 'goodness'. Others think it means 'conformity to the law's requirements.' Yet it seems clear that righteousness in this context is something to be received rather than achieved; and there is much to be said for taking it not in an ethical but in a soteriological sense. In 'Second Isaiah', as in the Psalms, 'righteousness' is very often a synonym for 'salvation'. It describes the activity of God whereby he vindicates the right. This meaning fits excellently here. The men of this Beatitude will then be those who 'follow after righteousness' (Isa. 51.1), who long for the 'coming right' of God's people and cause. We might paraphrase it: 'Blessed are those who ardently desire the vindication of the right, the triumph of the good cause.'

They shall be filled. They shall see the victory of God and good. Of that triumph we Christians have the first-fruits in the Cross and Resurrection. For us, in Cullmann's phrase, D-Day has been fought and won and it is the pledge of the final Victory-Day of God and right.

7 *The Fifth Beatitude.*

Mercy, an attribute of God himself' and something he 'requires' of man (Micah 6.8), is one of the great words of the Old Covenant which Christ takes over and writes in letters of gold in the charter of the New. 'Be ye merciful, even as your Father is merciful' (Luke 6.36). Mercy is the lovely virtue of the Good Samaritan (Luke 10.37); it is one of 'the weightier matters of the law' (Matt. 23.23); and lack of it will disqualify a man for God's forgiveness (Matt. 18.35). As Jesus construes it, mercy is always active: it is kindness in action, pity that clothes itself in gracious deeds, 'love to the loveless shown that they might lovely be'.[4]

They shall obtain mercy. From God's hands on Judgment Day. It is a striking fact that in the two parables in which Christ dwells on Judgment and the life beyond he singles out mercy—or the lack of it—as that which may decide a man's ultimate destiny (Luke 16.19-31; Matt. 25.31-46).

[4] 'The Red Cross spirit in the world' (Buttrick).

It is scarcely necessary to add that Jesus' meaning is not: 'Do merciful deeds, and you will establish a claim on God's mercy.' This is no 'merit' theology. To be merciful is the divine way of doing things; and if on Judgment Day the merciful man hears the verdict, 'Come, ye blessed of my Father', it will not be because he has 'made out, and reckoned on his ways, and bargained for his love', but because, all unconsciously, he has acted like him of whom it is written, 'as is his majesty, so also is his mercy'.

8 *The Sixth Beatitude*

Who is worthy to stand in the presence of God? Centuries before the Psalmist had answered, 'He that hath clean hands and a pure heart' (Ps. 24.3f). But the scribes and Pharisees of our Lord's time were prone to 'cleanse the outside of the cup, while the inside was full of evil' (Luke 11.39). Jesus lays all the stress on *inner* cleanness, knowing well that

> The heart aye's the part aye
> That makes us right or wrang.

Yet to be 'pure in heart' does not mean to be clean of every stain of sin, i.e. morally perfect. Jesus who came to call sinners, knew that none of us is sinless. Purity of heart stands rather for single-mindedness or sincerity. It is, in Temple's definition, 'a passionate aspiration towards the holiness of God'.

What does it mean to 'see God'? Since 'no man hath ever seen God', it is not a matter of optics but of spiritual fellowship. It is 'to be near God, and to know him, and to rejoice in him, all in one' (Montefiore). To enjoy such fellowship, says Jesus, a man must be wholly sincere. 'There are moral conditions for spiritual vision.'

The promise, however, is not exhausted by this life. Here 'we see through a glass darkly'—our finest vision is like looking at a distorted reflection in a brazen mirror—

but then 'face to face'. The final reward for the pure in
heart is 'the Beatific Vision' when, all veils of sin and sense
removed, 'they shall see his face' (Rev. 22.4). And that is
an experience which only one who is both great saint and
great poet may try to describe, and then only in utterly
inadequate symbol.

9   *The Seventh Beatitude.*

The Greek word *eirenopoioi* should be taken in its active
sense of 'peace-making', not in the passive one of 'peace-
able'. It is the peace-makers, not the peace-keepers whom
Christ blesses. The men Christ has in mind are not those
who purchase peace at any price but those who actively
reconcile and enlarge the area of human goodwill. By so
doing, they prove their moral kinship to the God of peace
(Rom. 15.33; Phil. 4.7, 9). Rabbi Hillel was not far from
the Kingdom when he said: 'Be of the disciples of Aaron,
loving peace and pursuing peace' (Aboth 1.2).

For they shall be called sons of God. No doubt Jesus
is looking away to the great Day of Judgment when God
shall pronounce this highest of all titles upon them. Yet
even now, as St Paul says, Christians are, potentially, 'sons
of God' in Christ (Rom. 8.14ff.) of which the Spirit in their
hearts, moving them to cry 'Abba, Father', is witness.
What will happen at the great Day will be a confirming of
their present dignity.

10   *The Eighth Beatitude.*

The Beatitude of the martyr, echoed in I Peter 3.14.
Righteousness probably means here the triumph of God's
good cause embodied in Jesus his Messiah. (In vss. 11-12,
a doublet of this verse, the persecution is 'for my sake'.)
Jesus, the Servant Messiah, knows that suffering will be the
lot of the Servant's disciples, but bids them 'count it all joy'
for the Kingdom of Heaven's sake. He does not mean that
suffering *qua* suffering is blessed: he means that where per-

secution needs must be, the disciple has an opportunity of proving his fitness for that Kingdom,

> Its king a servant, and its sign
> A gibbet on a hill.

11-12 This doublet of vs. 10 comes from Q, the second person plural replacing the third. The word 'falsely', omitted by the Western text, is probably a gloss. The Matthaean and the Lucan versions show variations:

(1) Matthew lists three kinds of persecution, Luke four.
(2) For Matthew's 'for my sake', Luke has 'for the Son of man's sake'. These variations do not affect the general sense. 'Say all manner of evil against you' (Matt.) and 'cast out your name as evil' (Luke) are variant translations of the underlying Aramaic.

Reproach, persecution and slander will be the lot of the Servant's disciples; but instead of fuming and fretting against their destiny, they are to be glad in hardship, remembering that such suffering has ever been the portion of 'his servants the prophets' and sure that a divine reward is theirs.

This, says the Jew Montefiore, strikes a new note. Joy in suffering has been distinctive of Christianity and of its saints and apostles and martyrs. And doubtless many thousands of humble sufferers have risen superior to their troubles and afflictions through the memory and influence of the Beatitudes.'[5]

But why, say the critics of Christianity, spoil it all by introducing the idea of 'reward'? So let us pause to consider our Lord's teaching about it.

The Doctrine of Reward.

A true man, says the objector, should believe in virtue for virtue's sake. All talk of reward, here or hereafter,

[5] *The Synoptic Gospels*[2], II, 44.

savours of the *quid pro quo* morality—the 'contract' idea of religion—which disfigured Judaism at its worst and from which Christians have not always kept themselves free. How shall we answer?

We all dislike the suggestion of the hymn:

> Whatever, Lord, we lend to Thee
> Repaid a thousand-fold will be.

Should we not rather agree:

> My God, I love Thee; not because
> I hope for heaven thereby,
> Nor yet for fear that loving not
> I might for ever die?

Yet that does not mean that we should wholly reject the idea of reward. Indeed, in a universe directed to moral ends good action and character must issue in some kind of satisfaction; and in the highest ethical systems it is arguable that there must be satisfactions. The real questions are: What is to be the nature of the rewards? And how far are they held out as inducements—as bribes?[6]

Tried by these tests, our Lord's doctrine has nothing to fear. It does not make the Christian life a mercenary affair. There are, as C. S. Lewis says,[7] rewards and rewards. 'There is the reward which has no natural connexion with the things you do to earn it, and is quite foreign to the desires that ought to accompany these things. Money is not the natural reward of love; that is why we call a man mercenary if he marries a woman for the sake of her money. But marriage is the proper reward for a real lover, and he is not mercenary for desiring it. A general who fights well in order to get a peerage is mercenary; a general who fights for victory is not, victory being the proper reward of battle as marriage is the proper reward of love. The proper

[6] C. A. Scott, *New Testament Ethics,* 52.
[7] See his sermon 'Weight of Glory' in *Transposition and other Addresses.*

rewards are not simply tacked on to the activity for which they are given, but are the activity itself in consummation.' So it is with the Christian doctrine of reward. The rewards offered by Jesus to the righteous are simply the inevitable issue of goodness in a world ruled over by a good God. Those who have attained to the Beatific Vision know that it is no mere bribe but simply the fit consummation of their their earthly communion with God.

We cannot then allow the word 'reward' to disappear from our Christian vocabulary. Jesus does say that God does not allow himself to be served in vain. On the other hand, his doctrine of reward is utterly un-mercenary:

First, Jesus repudiates the doctrine of 'merit', i.e. all suggestion that man can have a claim, as of right, on a Divine reward. For conclusive proof of this we need do no more than study the parables of the Farmer and his Man (Luke 17.7-10) and the Labourers in the Vineyard (Matt. 20.1-16)—well re-named by Jeremias 'The Good Employer'. This last especially destroys the reward idea while engaged in using it. Reward is a gift of God's grace.

Second, Jesus promises reward to those who are obedient without thought of reward. 'Do good,' he says (Luke 6.35), 'expecting nothing in return, and your reward will be great.' And in the parable of the Last Judgment (Matt. 25.31-46), which has been called the Story of the Great Surprises, 'the blessed of the Father' are rewarded just because they served and helped the needy with no thought of recompense.

Finally, the reward promised, which incidentally is the same for all, is the Kingdom of God—God's saving presence and fellowship, here and hereafter. And we may add that the clear implication of parables like the Talents is that the reward for a trusted servant is greater responsibility and closer fellowship with his Master (Matt. 25.23).

Paul once referred to 'the reward of grace' (Rom. 4.4), contrasting it with every reward of works to which men may lay claim. The phrase epitomizes Christ's concept of reward. Detached from all works of merit, reward is a matter of that divine grace and justice on which man must ever lean in faithful obedience.

A. THE LIFE DESCRIBED

(b) Its influence: Salt and Light. 5.13-16 M. Cf. Luke 14.34f.; 11.33, and Mark 9.50.

13 Ye are the salt of the earth: but if the salt have lost its savour, wherewith shall it be salted? It is thenceforth good for nothing, but to be cast out and trodden under foot of men.

14 Ye are the light of the world: a city set on a hill cannot
15 be hid. Neither do men light a lamp, and put it under the bushel, but on the stand, and it shineth unto all that are in
16 the house. Even so let your light shine before men, that they may see your good works, and glorify your Father which is in heaven.

In these little parables of salt and light Jesus describes the role which his disciples, the new Israel, are to play in the world.

13 *Ye are the salt of the earth.* Salt was precious in Palestine for preserving food, and it is probably its preservative power which Jesus has chiefly in mind. Applied to the disciples, it must signify their zeal, their devotion to their high task. By it God means to save and preserve the world. *But if the salt have lost its savour.* A solemn warning. The disciples had no doubt tasted salt from the Dead Sea which, having been adulterated with other minerals, had lost its astringent savour—had become insipid—and was thrown into the street as worthless. Insipid salt—disciples who have lost their zeal and devotion—a Judas who betrays his Master, a Demas forsaking the Gospel for the world—what could be more tragically useless? *Wherewith shall it be salted?* The corruption of the best is ever the worst. There is no remedy for it when God's salt goes bad. If the Church fails the world, what then? If Christ's men lose their characteristic tang—their fidelity to the Gospel, their loyalty to their Lord—then the world is on the road to spiritual decay.

14 *Ye are the light of the world.* Light stands for 'revelation', the saving knowledge of God, of which the disciples are to be the bearers. Centuries before, Isaiah had described the destiny of the Servant of the Lord thus:

> So I will make you a light of the nations
> That my salvation may reach to the end of the earth
> (Isa. 49.6).

Now Jesus and his disciples have been chosen by God to do what Israel had failed to do—'to be the sacred school of the knowledge of God for all mankind' (Athanasius).[8] Having kindled their torches at him who is 'the Light of the World' (John 8.12) his disciples are to be themselves a light to lead all men to God's truth. This is the Galilean command to world mission.

A city set on a hill cannot be hid. Let the disciples not imagine they can remain obscure. God has set them in a place of prominence, like some city crowning the sky-line and drawing the gaze of all. Less than a generation later Paul could say grimly that the apostles had become 'a spectacle to the world, to angels and to men' (I Cor. 4.9).

15 The parable of the Lamp has its parallels in Luke 11.33 and Mark 4.21. As lamps of the Lord, in whom God has kindled his light, the disciples must make their light available *for all that are in the house*—for the whole family of God. (Luke's version, 'that they which enter may see the light', suggests the influx of the Gentiles.) As no one hides the lit lamp under the upturned *bushel*, or 'meal tub', so

[8] *De Incarnatione*, xii.

the Gospel is not to be hidden or hoarded: it is to be broadcast.

16 *Even so let your light shine before men.* Your light means 'the light entrusted to you'. The disciples are to let it shine, through them, on the world, not for their own glory but for God's, who gave the light and who inspires all their good works. For men, as Bengel observes, are to see 'not the lamp but the shining', and give God the praise.

These parables are a perpetual rebuke to all Christians who suppose either that they can, like hermits, withdraw from the world, or that, entering it, they can conceal their true allegiance. Though the Christian is to be 'not of the world', he must be 'in it'—in it not only to be good but to do good and to influence others by his goodness, which is God's.

B. THE RELATION OF THE NEW ORDER TO THE OLD

Christ and the Old Order. 5.17-20 M.

17 Think not I came to destroy the law or the prophets: I
18 came not to destroy but to fulfil. For verily I say unto you, Till heaven and earth pass away, one jot or one tittle shall in no wise pass from the law, till all things be
19 accomplished. Whosoever therefore shall break one of these least commandments and shall teach men so, shall be called least in the kingdom of heaven: but whosoever shall do and teach them, he shall be called great in the
20 kingdom of heaven. For I say unto you, that except your righteousness exceed the righteousness of the scribes and Pharisees, ye shall in no wise enter the kingdom of heaven.

What is the relation of the New Order (the Kingdom of God) to the Old Order of the Law and the Prophets? Does it annul and abolish it? No, says Jesus, the New Order is the 'fulfilment' of the Old, its crown and completion; and the moral demands of the New Order 'exceed' those taught by scribe and Pharisee.

This summarizes vss. 17 and 20. Between them lie the hardest verses in the Sermon. Consider what they say: 'The Law, down to its last dotted "i" and stroked "t" will last to the end of time. If anyone breaks one of its least important commands, he will get the lowest rank in God's realm. The highest place will go to the man who both teaches and himself observes them.'

These verses, as they stand, can hardly be words of Christ; for (a) the doctrine of the Law's permanence is pure rabbinism; and (b) Jesus himself 'relaxed' the Sabbath law, annulled the law about purity, and rejected Moses' command about divorce. They read, rather, like some early Jewish Christian misapplication of some words of Jesus. Thus, vs. 18 has its parallel in Luke 16.17, 'It is easier for heaven and earth to pass away than for one tittle of the law to fall'. This, as T. W. Manson[9] suggests, is an ironic comment by Jesus on the unbending conservatism of the scribes. 'The world will end sooner than you scribes will give up the tiniest bit of tradition by which you make the law of no effect.' What we have in Matthew is Christian legalism such as may have arisen in ultra-conservative circles which were shocked by the attitude of Paul and his friends to the Law.

Turn back to vss. 17 and 20. The purpose of his coming (Jesus says) is not to 'scrap' the ancient revelation, but to complete it. True religion, presented as an ideal in the Old Testament, is now realized with the coming of the Kingdom, and the Gospel is the fulfilment of Old Testament prophecy. Scribe and Pharisee had externalized, had legalized, the old revelation of God's will. The demands

[9] *The Sayings of Jesus,* 135. In *Jesus Then and Now* Dr William Lillie takes these vexatious verses to be a hyperbolic saying of Jesus in which he asserts that his whole mission and message are firmly grounded in the Old Testament revelation.

of the Kingdom are more radical. The will of God, as interpreted by his Messiah, demands a morality in the blood and bone; it calls for truth in the inward parts, as the succeeding six antitheses will show.

18 *Jot . . . tittle. Jot* is the Greek *iota*, equivalent to *yodh*, the smallest letter in the Hebrew alphabet. *Tittle* (Gr. *keraia*) probably means a decorative 'stroke' or 'crown' attached by the scribes to certain Hebrew letters (Strack-Billerbeck, *Kommentar*, I, 248).

C. ITS OUTWORKINGS

(a) In thought, word and deed. 5.21-48.

Jesus now proceeds to expound the 'higher righteousness' of the Kingdom of God. Six times he quotes the provision of the old Law. Six times with his sovereign 'But I say unto you' he sets over against it the divine ideal of the men of the Kingdom. The Messiah demands something far more radical than Moses; and as he deepens, completes, exposes the profoundest implications of the ancient directives, we see that 'Jesus understands the Old Testament better than the Old Testament itself'.

Critical analysis suggests that underlying vss. 21-48 is a little sermon of Jesus which St Matthew has expanded with other sayings of Jesus. The kernel was probably six brief antitheses comprising vss. 21-22a, 27-28, 31-32, 33-34a, 38-39a, 43-44a. We might set them down thus:

The old Law said, 'No murder'. I say, 'No anger'.

The old Law said, 'No adultery'. I say, 'No lustful thought'.

The old Law said, 'Divorce on condition . . . ' I say, 'No Divorce'.

The old Law said, 'No false swearing'. I say, 'No swearing at all'.

The old Law said, 'Eye for eye'. I say, 'No retaliation at all'.

The old Law said, 'Love your neighbour'. I say, 'Love your enemy'.

Some have called this 'the new Law of the Messiah'. Let us beware how we use the word 'law'. Laws, as we understand the word, are founded on a calculation of how most men may reasonably be expected to act. The assumption is that with a reasonable effort men may keep them. But if Christ's commands are laws of this kind, who is sufficient for them? No anger, no lust, no swearing, no retaliation—who can rise to the height of these demands? If our salvation depends on our perfect keeping of these 'laws', we are all doomed to be damned, and Christ is laying on his disciples a burden far heavier than the scribes and Pharisees did on theirs. This cannot be legislation. To be sure, this is how God means men to live; but though all who call themselves Christ's disciples must try to live according to this pattern, none of us who live in a fallen world dare claim, 'All these have I kept'. More clearly than any other part of the Sermon, these verses at once declare the Christian moral ideal and convict us of our sin. We may, with Paul, give thanks to God that we are saved not by law but by grace.

21-26 *Murder.* M+Q. (25-26=Luke 12.58f.)

21   Ye have heard that it was said to them of old time, Thou shalt not kill; and whosoever shall kill shall be in danger
22   of the judgment: but I say unto you, that every one who is angry with his brother[10] shall be in danger of the judgment; and whosoever shall say to his brother Raca, shall be in danger of the council; and whosoever shall
23   say, Thou fool, shall be in danger of the hell of fire. If therefore thou art offering thy gift at the altar, and there rememberest that thy brother hath aught against thee,

[10] The words 'without a cause' ($\epsilon i \kappa \hat{\eta}$), read by the AV, are not read by some of our best MSS and are probably a gloss.

24 leave there thy gift before the altar, and go thy way, first
    be reconciled to thy brother, and then come and offer thy
    gift.
25 Agree with thine adversary quickly, whiles thou art with
    him in the way; lest haply the adversary deliver thee to
    the judge, and the judge deliver thee to the officer, and
26 thou be cast into prison. Verily I say unto thee, thou shalt
    by no means come out thence, till thou have paid the last
    farthing.

21f. To the first antithesis Matthew has added a saying
about reconciliation and the parable of the defendant.

Jesus begins with the sixth commandment, which pro-
hibits murder. Murder, he says, under the Old Order was
liable to trial and punishment as prescribed in the Law—
in this case, death (Ex. 21.12; Lev. 24.17). In the New
Order, he says, not merely the overt act of murder but the
inward passion of anger will expose a man to judgment,
i.e. by God. This is really the end of the antithesis.

The following words are very puzzling. *Raca* (*rēkā*) is
probably an Aramaic abuse-word meaning 'blockhead'.[11]
But why should one abusive word get legal treatment only,
the other eschatological? Perhaps the original form of 22bc
was this: '(It was said to the men of old), Whoever says
"Blockhead" to his brother shall be liable to the council
(Sanhedrin): (but I say unto you), Whoever says to his
brother "fool" shall be liable to hell fire.'

23f. *If therefore thou art offering thy gift at the altar.*
No act of worship is acceptable to God so long as the wor-
shipper is on bad terms with his brother. We must get right
with our fellow-man before we go into the presence of God.
Christ speaks to Jews: but he speaks also to Christians.
We too 'have an altar'. The Table and Cup of the Lord are

[11] It should be added that *Raca* may be the vocative of a *Greek*
abusive word $\rho\alpha\chi\hat{\alpha}s$ found in a papyrus; similarly, $\mu\omega\rho\acute{e}$ may trans-
transliterate a rabbinic word *mōrā* 'outcast'.

truly, as 'Rabbi' Duncan said, 'for sinners'. Yet it behoves us to purge our hearts of hatred towards our fellow-man before we dare to keep the feast of him who is our peace.

25f. The point of the parable of the Defendant, *in this context,* is similar. 'Never leave a quarrel unmade-up.' But Matthew derives the parable from Q, and in its Lucan setting (Luke 12.58f.) the meaning seems to be: 'Get right with God now, before the day of reckoning comes,' i.e. the destruction of the Jewish nation which Jesus predicted.

27-30   *Adultery.* M. Cf. Mark 9.43-48; Matt. 18.8-9.

27 Ye have heard that it was said, Thou shalt not commit
28 adultery: but I say unto you, that every one that looketh
    on a woman to lust after her hath committed adultery
    already with her in his heart.
29 And if thy right eye causeth thee to stumble,
        pluck it out, and cast it from thee:
    For it is profitable for thee that one of thy members
        should perish,
        and not thy whole body be cast into hell.
30 And if thy right hand causeth thee to stumble,
        cut it off and cast it from thee;
    For it is profitable for thee that one of thy members
        should perish,
        and not thy whole body go into hell.

To this second antithesis Matthew has added some words of Jesus about self-discipline quoted independently by Mark (9.43-48).

27f. From the sixth commandment Jesus turns to the seventh. 'Thou shalt not commit adultery,' said the old Law. 'Even the lustful look,' says Jesus, 'is sin.'

In Jewish law adultery meant intercourse with the wife or the betrothed of a Jew. Jesus evidently applies the word to illicit intercourse with any woman. The man in question looks on the woman *in order to* lust after her. The Greek idiom used shows that Jesus means not the involuntary waking of the sexual impulse but the deliberate intent to sin. Lack of opportunity may restrain him from actual sin; but in intention he has already committed the act. Thus deliberately to will to sin has, in Jesus' view, the guilt of sin.

Jesus is not condemning normal and lawful sexual desire. 'What he condemns is the regarding of a woman simply as a means for the gratification of our desires—as an object and not as a person. This is the root evil in adultery (and prostitution) which are only the external expressions of this state of mind.'[12]

29f. The sayings about the offending eye and hand are figurative and hyperbolical. (After all, the removal of eye or hand would not remove the sinful thought in the heart.) But they teach a very important principle—that a man's salvation may depend on rigorous self-discipline. The danger for us is that, having decided that the words are not to be taken literally, we may dilute all the rigour out of them. If Jesus' teaching does not mean that we are to amputate one or other of our limbs, it *may* mean for any one of us the removal of a salacious book or of an evil friendship from our lives. So too with Jesus' language about 'hell'. If we say that the language about 'going to hell' is metaphorical, it is metaphor which signifies something terribly real. As being 'in heaven' means being 'in the presence of God', so being in hell means being utterly separate from him, which is spiritual death. Better, says Jesus, to live a maimed life than with all your faculties to suffer such a death.

[12] A. D. Lindsay, *The Moral Teaching of Jesus*, 145.

31-32 *Divorce.* M. Cf. Mark 10.2-12; Matt. 19.1-12; Luke 16.18; I Cor. 7.10f.

31 It was also said, Whosoever shall put away his wife, let
32 him give her a writing of divorcement: but I say unto you, that every one that putteth away his wife, saving for the cause of fornication, maketh her an adulteress: and whosoever shall marry her when she is put away committeth adultery.

Jesus' teaching on marriage and divorce raises many questions. What did he actually say? Was he laying down a law or stating an ideal? How far is his teaching practicable for us?

It is best to begin with Jesus' discussion of the Mosaic law on marriage in Mark 10.2-12.

The Mosaic Law (Deut. 24.1) lays it down that a man may divorce his wife if 'she finds no favour in his eyes, because he hath found some unseemly thing in her'. The man must then give her a certificate of divorce, and she is free to go and marry another. But what constitutes an 'unseemly thing'? In our Lord's time the rabbis could not agree. Shammai and his disciples took it to mean some grave offence like adultery. Hillel and his followers held that a man could divorce his wife for no more serious misdemeanour than 'letting his food burn'. It was against the background of this dispute that a Pharisee asked Jesus, 'Is it lawful for a man to divorce his wife?'

In his reply Jesus did three things. First, he described the law of Moses as a concession to human hardheartedness. Second, quoting Gen. 2.23-24, he reaffirmed the divine ideal of marriage as an indissoluble union—physical and spiritual—of man and wife. Third, he condemned re-marriage after divorce.

(Notice that in Jewish law, while a woman could commit adultery against her husband, a husband could not commit adultery against his wife. In the Marcan passage Jesus denies this, putting the sexes on a level.)

We may now return to Matt. 5.31-32. Here Jesus apparently finds one valid reason for divorce, viz., unchastity or, as we should say, 'misconduct' (though whether the words covers pre-marital unchastity as well as adultery is not certain). But does this 'exceptive clause' go back to Jesus? We may gravely doubt it. For (1) if it does, Jesus is simply taking sides with Shammai against Hillel in the current dispute; (2) neither Mark nor Luke nor Paul seems to know anything about it: and (3) in Matt. 19.9 where the exception also occurs, Matthew has clearly inserted it into his Marcan source. Probably therefore the clause is a later addition by some Christians who found Christ's teaching too rigorous to apply in certain cases.

The truth seems to be that Jesus was not laying down a binding law about marriage but stating the divine ideal. (If this saying is a piece of legislation, it stands alone in the Sermon!) Marriage, in Jesus' view, is a God-given institution, having for its aim the life-long union of a man and a woman, and divorce is a declension from the divine will for them.

But if Jesus stated the ideal, he did not go into the casuistry of the matter. What guidance can we draw from Jesus' teaching for the solution of the many thorny problems that face the Church to-day? This much we may venture to say. First, it is marriage between disciples— Christian marriage, as we should call it—that he has in mind. We Christians have no right to regard it as a law and demand that it be put in the statute books of the nation. In other words, in this sinful world where hardness of heart still survives, and where so many have not the smallest desire to take the divine ideal seriously, the ideal cannot be made compulsory. 'A view of marriage voluntarily adopted *within* the Kingdom of God cannot be enforced by legal sanctions *outside*.' Second, within the Christian society we must ensure that the divine ideal is honoured and upheld, recognizing that divorce is a grave departure from God's will. We must do all that we may to see that a marriage vow, once undertaken, shall not be broken; and we may discern in Christ's warning against re-marriage his desire that wide room should be left for the chance of repentance and reconciliation.

33-37 *Oaths.* M.

33   Again ye have heard that it was said to them of old time,
       Thou shalt not forswear thyself, but shalt perform unto the
34   Lord thine oaths: but I say unto you. Swear not at all;
           neither by the heaven,
               for it is the throne of God;
35   nor by the earth,
               for it is the footstool of his feet;
           nor by Jerusalem,
               for it is the city of the great King.
36   Neither shalt thou swear by thy head,
               for thou canst not make one hair white or black.
37   But let your speech be, Yea, yea; Nay, nay;
               and whatsoever is more than these is of the evil one.

What is an oath? It is a solemn invoking of God as witness to the truth of a statement. Oaths arise because men are so often liars. The theory behind them is that there are two kinds of statement: the first, fortified by an oath, which must be fulfilled; the other which, lacking the oath, need not be fulfilled.

The Jews were fond of oaths, as all Orientals are to this day—and many Occidentals too! The Law permitted them, but warned against false swearing (Lev. 19.12; Ex. 20.7, etc.). Some oaths involving the name of God were said to be binding; others which brought in 'heaven' or 'earth' were not so. Only the Essenes avoided oaths completely, as the Quakers do to-day.

Jesus sweeps away 'the whole mechanics of swearing'. Do men suppose that when they take an oath they are putting themselves into the presence of God? Men, if they but knew it, are always in God's presence. Therefore, for the men of the Kingdom, Jesus lays down the principle of pure truthfulness—truth on the lips and truth in the heart. A plain Yes or a plain No, he says, is enough. To interpret Jesus' words as an absolute prohibition of an oath in any circumstances, as the Anabaptists, the Quakers and Tolstoy have done, is to confound the letter with the spirit. Once again, it is the principle that matters: this is not a law.

34f. *Heaven . . . earth . . . Jerusalem.* All these things imply God who made them and rules over them. To swear by them is simply a specious evasion of swearing 'by God'.

36 *Swear by the head.* To swear by the head or by the hair on it was common then, as it still is in Syria. 'I remember distinctly,' writes Mr Rihbany, himself a modern Syrian, 'how proud I was in my youth to put my hand on my moustache, when it was not yet even large enough to be respectfully noticed, and swear by it as a man.[13] How absurd, says Jesus of such an oath, to swear by a bit of himself over which he has not the slightest proprietorship! God only has power over the colour of a man's hair: it is he who ordains the raven locks of youth, the white hair of old age.

37 James 5.12 gives a clearer version of this saying: 'Let your Yea be Yea, and your Nay be Nay.' *The evil one.* Satan. But the Greek may equally well mean 'the evil' (that is in the world).

38-42 *Retaliation.* M + Q. Cf. Luke 6.29-3.

38 Ye have heard that it was said, An eye for an eye, and a tooth for a tooth;

[13] *The Syrian Christ*, 122.

39 But I say unto you, Resist not him that is evil:
    but whosoever smiteth thee on thy right cheek,
        turn to him the other also.
40 And if any man would go to law with thee, and take away
        thy coat,
    let him have thy cloak also.
41 And whosoever shall compel thee to go one mile,
        go with him twain.
42 Give to him that asketh thee,
    and from him that would borrow of thee turn not thou
        away.

The old Law said 'eye for eye' (Ex. 21.23-25; Lev. 24.17-21; Deut. 19.16-21). True, there is some evidence that in our Lord's time a monetary fine replaced the literal enforcement of the law; but the *lex talionis*, the law of measure for measure, was the basis of Greek and Roman law also, and indeed goes back almost 2,000 years before Christ to the Code of Hammurabi. But, for Jesus, it is not God's way and therefore cannot be the ideal for the men of the Kingdom.

Let us, however, watch the translation of vs. 39. The AV has 'resist not evil'; the RV 'resist not him that is evil'. But the NEB translation probably brings out Jesus' meaning best: 'Do not set yourself up against the man who wrongs you.' What Jesus had in mind was personal wrong, malicious injury inflicted by a personal enemy. 'Withstand not wrong' is what he means, 'Don't let it bring you into the ring.'[14]

The principle therefore which he enunciates is that of *non-retaliation in cases of personal wrong*, and he drives it home with four picturesque illustrations. One is a personal assault; another, a suit at law; a third, an official demand; and the fourth, a request for help. Interpret these illustrations as laws to be obeyed to the letter, and we miss the point. Literal obedience to them would only result in violence, robbery and anarchy. For Jesus is here talking to

[14] C. A. Scott, *New Testament Ethics*, 61f.

disciples, and speaking of personal relations: he is not laying down moral directives for states and nations, and such issues as the work of the police or the question of a defensive war are simply not in his mind.

Well then, it may be asked, does this doctrine of Jesus work in the sphere of personal relations? To this question we may reply with another, Do we ever cure injustice by violent retaliation? If you hit a man back when he hits you, who is benefited? Of course, revenge is sweet—to the natural man. The man of the Kingdom knows that revenge is poison, that it only breeds endless ill feeling and bitterness. On the other hand, there are cases without number where Jesus' principle is justified to the hilt, and good people do carry it out. Not to retort on rudeness with rudeness, to stifle an angry reply to an insult, to forgive an injury—is not this to act on Christ's principle, and does not such an action bring blessing into our discordant human life? 'We can never know,' comments Montefiore, 'how much hot anger has been quelled, how much lust for vengeance has been suppressed, how much self-sacrifice has been evoked, by the paradoxical, stimulating and pictures doctrine of "the other cheek" and of "the coat and the cloak".'[15]

Let us deal with the details of the illustrations in the notes.

39 The saying about 'the other cheek' has humour in it.

'If a man smite thee on the one cheek'—a pause while each man thought furiously what was to be done. But Jesus' completion of his sentence must have staggered them completely, 'Well, you have another!'[16] Matthew mentions 'the right cheek', probably on purpose. According to the rabbis, a blow with the back of the hand which would normally land on your opponent's right cheek, was twice as bad as

[15] *Op. cit.,* 71.
[16] W. R. Maltby, *The Significance of Jesus,* 82.

hitting him with the flat of your hand. Notice too that the words of this verse recall Isa. 51.6 which describes the behaviour of the Servant of the Lord towards his persecutors. This is no accident. The disciples of the Servant Son of God are called on to live in the spirit of the Servant. Cf. Mark 10.42-45.

40 Second illustration, this time from the law-court. The opponent sues for the recovery of a 'shirt'. 'Give him your coat too,' says Jesus. A man who obeyed this literally would find himself practically nude—clear proof that Jesus is illustrating a principle, not framing a law.

41 Third illustration, an official demand. The Greek word *angareuō* underlying the English 'compel' goes back to the Persian Royal Mail. The *angaros* was a courier in the King's service empowered to 'commandeer' or 'conscript' other people in his service. So the verb came to signify forced labour, and in Christ's time it would generally mean a Roman official saying to a Jew, 'Here! Shoulder this bit of baggage, and get moving!' or some such similar request. (Cf. Mark 15.21. The Roman soldiers 'impressed' Simon of Cyrene to carry Jesus' cross.) When that happens, says Jesus, and you have done the mile he demanded, disarm him completely by carrying his bag another mile. 'The first mile renders to Caesar the things that are Caesar's; the second mile, by meeting oppression with kindness, renders to God the things that are God's.' (T. W. Manson.)[17]

42 *Prima facie*, this is an exhortation to indiscriminate almsgiving. And we all know to what evils that may lead. (It is said that the saintly William Law gave away £2,500 per annum to beggars in his backyard—and succeeded in demoralizing the neighbourhood.) Once again, it is the principle that is important—the principle of generous giving.

[17] *The Sayings of Jesus*, 160.

43-48   *Love.*   Q + M.   Cf. Luke 6.27-28, 32-36.

43   Ye have heard that it was said, Thou shalt love thy neigh-
44   bour and hate thine enemy: but I say unto you, Love your
45   enemies and pray for them that persecute you, that ye
     may be sons of your Father which is in heaven:
>   For he maketh his sun to rise on the evil and the good
>   and sendeth rain on the just and the unjust.
46   For if ye love them that love you, what reward have ye?
>   Do not even the publicans the same?
47   And if ye salute your brethren only, what do ye more than
     others?
>   Do not even the Gentiles the same?
48   Ye therefore shall be perfect as your heavenly Father is
     perfect.

The 'new righteousness' culminates in the command to
'love your enemies'. The Old Order had demanded that the
Jew love his fellow-Jew. The New Order demands that the
new Israel should love without a limit. So will they prove
themselves sons of their Father whose grace in nature does
not distinguish between good and bad. A love such as the
tax-gatherers and Gentiles show, which rises no higher than
the morality of 'one good turn deserves another', is not
enough. Complete catholicity in love—like God's—is the
ideal Christ sets before his disciples.

What does Jesus mean by 'love' (*agapē*)? In our language
love is a word 'soiled by all ignoble use' and by erotic and
sentimental associations. Love, for Jesus, is not emotion;
neither does he mean 'you must resolve to like' certain
people. He does not mean that we should 'love' all and
sundry in the same sense as we love our nearest and dearest.
For Jesus, 'love' means practical and persistent goodwill
towards all men: it means 'caring' for others, and seeking
their good. (Cf. Von Hügel's dying words[18]: 'Christianity
taught us to care. Caring is the greatest thing. Caring matters most.') In this sense we may 'love' others whom we do

[18] *Letters to a Niece*, xliii.

not 'like'. And we are to 'care' for others, because 'caring' is God's way.

This is the crown of our Lord's teaching about love. In Mark 12.28f. he sets love of one's neighbour second only to love of God. In the parable of the Good Samaritan (Luke 10.30ff.) he refuses to set a limit to the scope of the word 'neighbour'. Here he carries things to their spiritually logical conclusion—the love of a persecuting enemy.

How far his followers have come short of this ideal, history only too sadly bears witness. When a Jew like Montefiore can declare that 'the adherents of no religion have hated their enemies more than Christians', we may think he goes too far; yet we must confess that the attitude of Christians to Christ's 'kinsmen after the flesh' down the centuries has been a great betrayal of him who died with a prayer for the forgiveness of his enemies. If we may justly be proud of a document which possesses such a command as this, we must ever hear sounding in our ears the terrible word of Christ to his disciples, 'Why do you call me Lord, Lord, and do not the things which I say?'

43 Thou shalt love thy neighbour. Lev. 19.18. *Neighbour* means fellow-Israelite. The actual words, 'Thou shalt hate thine enemy' do not occur in the Old Testament. Some hold that what Jesus said was simply:

> It was said, Thou shalt love thy neighbour:
> But I say unto you, Love your enemies.

In that case the words would be a later addition. The substance of the words is, however, found in OT passages like Deut. 23.6 and Ps. 139.21f.

44 Matthew has two imperatives: 'love' and 'pray'; Luke has four: 'love', 'do good', 'bless' and 'pray for'; and the last three show how *practically* Jesus interpreted the word 'love'.

45 *Sons*: in a moral sense. In a human family, if a son honours and obeys his father, he realizes his sonship. If he dishonours and disrespects him, he repudiates his sonship. So it is in the family of God.

46 For Matthew's 'what reward have ye?' Luke has 'What thank (*charis*) have ye?' A. D. Lindsay[19] comments: 'What does reward mean here? Isn't it like saying, "What is the fun of stopping short at loving people that love you"? Can't you see that it's more exciting than that?' *What do ye more?* Christ's doctrine of the extra. To return evil for good is the devil's way: to return good for good is man's: to return good for evil is God's.

48 For Matthew's 'perfect' Luke has 'merciful'. Some hold Luke to be the original. If Matthew's 'perfect', which is 'the harder reading', is preferred, to what are we summoned? Hardly to sinlessness, for Jesus knew that men are 'evil'. The sentence recalls Lev. 19.2. 'Ye shall be holy, for I the Lord your God am holy', with a clear echo of Deut. 18.13, 'Thou shalt be perfect (Heb. *tamim*, LXX *teleios*, as here) with the Lord thy God'. *Tamim* means whole, complete. The disciples of Jesus, then, are to be as complete or 'all-round' in their love as God is, who sends his sun and rain on good and bad alike. Torrey[20] reaches a like conclusion by a different way. He thinks the Aramaic word Jesus used was *g'mar* in its active sense of 'all-including'. We might then render: 'You therefore shall be catholic (in your love) as your heavenly Father is catholic.'

Catholic as God? Yes. Of course, the ideal is beyond us. Yet we should remember that we are not called to make the attempt in our own unaided strength. A story is told of a girl who was sure she could climb a certain mountain. But by and by, as the road steepened and narrowed, she

[19] *The Moral Teaching of Jesus*, 61.
[20] *The Four Gospels*, 291.

sank down exhausted. Then came her father, with his supporting arm to help her to the top. This is a parable: we are not left to climb that mountain alone.

C. ITS OUTWORKINGS

(b) In worship. 6.1-18.

What went before concerned the relations of man with his fellow-creatures. What follows concerns his relations with his Maker—with worship. Vss. 1-18 deal with three acts of worship: almsgiving, prayer and fasting.

The kernel of this section was a little sermon with three 'heads':

    2-4: almsgiving
    5-6: prayer
  16-18: fasting

each containing two 'refrains'—

> They have received their reward
> Thy Father which seeth in secret shall recompense thee.

St Matthew has expanded them with further sayings of Jesus, viz., 7-8 (on wrong praying), 9-13 (the disciples' prayer), and 14-15 (on forgiveness).

The principle which Jesus lays down in all three cases is the same, and it applies to every sort of religious observance. The thing that matters is sincerity before God, as the cardinal sin is hypocrisy. He states the principle in the first verse: 'Your worship is for God's eyes alone, not men's.' All piety done to purchase human applause is rejected by God. The only worship he approves is that done in quiet secrecy, with no thought of gaining anything for one's self.

1-4 *Almsgiving.* M.

1 Take heed that ye do not your righteousness before men, to be seen of them: else ye have no reward with your Father which is in heaven.

2 When therefore thou doest alms,

>Sound not a trumpet before thee, as the hypocrites do in the synagogues and in the streets

>That they may have glory of men.

>Verily I say unto you, They have received their reward.

3 But when thou doest alms,

>Let not thy left hand know what thy right hand doeth,

4 That thine alms may be in secret:

>And thy Father which seeth in secret shall recompense thee.

The first illustration of the principle enunciated in verse 1 is from almsgiving. The Jews, who rightly counted it a part of worship, set great store by it. 'Blessed is he that considereth the poor,' said the Psalmist (Ps. 41.1); and the book of Tobit comes near to regarding it in the light of what has been cynically called 'fire insurance': 'It is better to give alms than to lay up gold: alms doth deliver from death, and it shall purge away all sin' (Tobit 12.8f.). The rabbis, to be sure, taught that almsgiving should be secret, one of them even asserting that 'he who gives alms in secret is greater than Moses'. But among the Jews, as among Christians to-day, were hypocrites who liked to publicize their charity in order to buy human credit. It is these 'humbugs' whom Jesus pillories. They get what they bargain for, he says, and that is all the reward they will ever get. The only charity which God approves is that which is done with complete unobtrusiveness, with no thought of the amount appearing in 'the parish magazine'. Jesus does not mean that secret charity which wins heavenly dividends pays better than publicized charity which buys only human applause. He means that the anonymous helping of one's brother is the only sort God rewards, precisely because the giver seeks nothing for himself.

2 *Sound not a trumpet.* Metaphorical. 'Don't publicize your piety.' *As the hypocrites do.* Hypocrisy means literally 'acting a part', and a hypocrite is a play-actor. The men condemned are those who wore a mask of piety over their selfish lives. Many were no doubt Pharisees—bad Pharisees; but we have no right to make the automatic equation: Pharisee = hypocrite, or suppose that the Pharisees had any monopoly of this sin. *They have received their reward.* The Greek verb employed here[21] occurs commonly in the papyri as a business formula of receipt such as a tax-collector might use: 'I have received.' So it is used here, with more than a touch of irony. 'These hypocrites,' says Jesus, 'can sign the receipt for their reward.' Their piety is a commercial transaction. They aim to buy men's applause, and they get it—there and then. And that is all the reward they are ever going to get. The account is closed.

3 *Let not thy left hand know what thy right hand doeth.* A vividly proverbial expression for close fellowship. We might say, 'Don't let your bosom crony know about your charity.'

4 *Thy Father which seeth in secret.* Either 'your Father who sees you, though you don't see him', or the Greek may conceal an Aramaic phrase meaning, 'your Father who sees what is secret', i.e. your secret charity. *Shall recompense thee.* In heaven, or at Judgment Day.

5-8 *Prayer.* M.

5   And when ye pray, ye shall not be as the hypocrites:
        for they love to stand and pray in the synagogues and
            in the corners of the streets,
        that they may be seen of men.
    Verily I say unto you, They have received their reward.

[21] ἀπέχω.

6   But thou, when thou prayest,
     enter into thine inner chamber, and having shut thy
        door, pray to thy Father which is in secret,
     and thy Father which seeth in secret shall recompense
        thee.
7   And in praying use not vain repetitions as the heathen do:
     for they think that they shall be heard for their much
        speaking.
8   Be not like unto them:
     for your Father knoweth what things ye have need of
        before you ask him.

The second illustration—from prayer.

The pious Jew, like the Moslem today, had his set times
of prayer (9 a.m., 12 noon and 3 p.m.); and just as the
Moslem when the muezzin is heard (or the Catholic when
the *Angelus* rings), gets down on his knees, wherever he
chances to be, so the Jew would halt in the street and
engage in prayer. Jesus will have none of it, not because set
times are bad, but because the practice too easily breeds
hypocrites who like to be 'alone with God', surrounded by
plenty of admiring spectators! This is hypocrisy; for while
he is supposedly praying to God, the hypocrite is really
'playing to the gallery'.

The secret of religion (says Jesus) is religion in secret.
The true man of prayer will seek a quiet place for his communion with God. Nor will he, like the pagan, bombard
the unseen world with empty babbling as though the virtue
of prayer lay in sheer verbosity, but will rest in faith on a
Father who knows all his children's needs already.

'How simple, fine and telling the words are,' comments
Montefiore,[22] ' "your Father knows what you need before
you ask him".' If the logician objects that prayer is useless,
because God knows all your needs already, we may reply:
first, that it is Jesus himself who bids us 'ask, seek and
knock'; second, that prayer is needful on man's account,

[22] *Op. cit.*, II, 99.

for even in a human family the child must ask, though his father is well aware of his needs; and third, that, as life is more than logic, so in the soul's communion with God we pass into a sphere where the writ of human reasoning does not run.

5f. Private prayers offered in public places, not 'church' prayers, are meant. The *inner chamber* (a phrase from Isa. 26.20) means any place apart. For Edward Wilson of the Antarctic it was the crow's nest on the *Terra Nova*—'my private chapel', as he called it in a letter to his wife.[23]

7 *Use not vain repetitions.* The Greek word (*battalogeō*) must mean 'babble' or 'gabble', but its etymology is uncertain. It may be an onomatopoeic verb meaning 'babble' like the Greek *battarizō*, 'stutter'; or akin to *battalos*, 'gabbler' (a nickname bestowed on Demosthenes); or the transliteration of two Aramaic words meaning 'speak empty things'. *Codex Bezae* has *blattalogeō* (Latin, *blatero*, English 'blather').

What kind of pagan 'babbling' has Jesus in mind? The pagan worships not one but many deities. He is not sure which one is best qualified to answer his prayer. So he heaps up the names and epithets of the various gods in the torrent of his prayer, in hope to 'get through' to the right one.

9-13 *The Disciples' Prayer.* M. Luke 11.2ff. (L).

9 After this manner there- fore pray ye:	
Our *Father* which art in heaven,	*Father.*
Hallowed be thy name:	*Hallowed be thy name,*
10 *Thy kingdom come:*	*Thy kingdom come.*
Thy will be done,	
As in heaven, so on earth.	
11 *Give us* this day *our* *daily bread,*	*Give us* day by day *our daily* *bread.*

[23] George Seaver, *Edward Wilson of the Antarctic*, 213.

12 *And forgive us our* debts,   *And forgive us our* sins,
    As *we also* have *forgiven*   For *we also forgive* every one
      our debtors,   that is indebted to us,
13 *And bring us not into*   *And bring us not into*
      temptation,   *temptation.*
    but deliver us from the
      evil one.

The differences between the two versions are these:

(1) Luke has nothing corresponding to 'Thy will be done,
    as in heaven, so on earth' or to 'but deliver us from the
    evil one'.

(2) For 'Our Father which
          art in heaven'   Luke has simply 'Father'.
        'this day'   Luke has 'day by day'.
        'debts'   Luke has 'sins'.

(3) There is a difference in the Greek tenses used by Matt.
    (*dos*: give) and Luke (*didou*: keep on giving) in the
    'bread' petition, as there is a slight variation in the
    'forgiveness' petition.

We should also note (1) that some MSS read 'Thy holy
Spirit come upon us and cleanse us' for 'Thy kingdom
come' in Luke's version; and (2) that the familiar Doxology,
though early, is no true part of the Prayer.

The differences have caused endless discussion. Some
have thought the two versions represent teaching given by
Jesus on two different occasions. Others explain them in
terms of independent translation from an original Aramaic
and of handing down in church circles over a period
of some forty years. The Form Critics have even
suggested that Matthew's version was that used at the
Eucharist and Luke's that used at Baptism and in small
groups.

Which has the better claim to preserve the mind of

Christ? Some take Luke's to be more original, and explain why Matthew has added this or that; others, preferring Matthew's, find reasons for Luke's omissions. It is wiser to admit that, as in the narratives of the Lord's Supper, no single fixed form has come down to us. The fact is that you can make out a case for either version. If it be urged that, since prayers tend to get longer rather than shorter in the process of transmission, Luke's briefer version must be nearer to Jesus, equally can it be urged that the well-rounded poetic structure and the Jewish traits of Matthew's are arguments on the other side. So with details. A strong case based on Jesus' own usage and Paul's testimony (Mark 14.36; Rom. 8.15; Gal. 4.6) can be urged for preferring Luke's 'Father' to Matthew's 'Our Father which art in heaven' (which was a current Jewish address of God). On the other hand, Matthew's versions of the 'bread' and the 'forgiveness' petitions seem superior to Luke's more generalized equivalents. What is certain is that the Church has always preferred Matthew's; and it is undoubtedly the smoother and more satisfying version.

In what sense is the Prayer original? Jewish scholars have been at great pains to parallel each clause of the Prayer from one Jewish source or another. Thus the very old *Kaddish* prayer has the words: 'May his great name be magnified and hallowed in the world.' The *Eighteen Benedictions*, another famous and ancient synagogue prayer, has: 'Forgive us, our Father, for we have sinned against thee.' And one, Dr Elbogen, by 'fishing in the Talmudic sea', has composed a patchwork prayer of one hundred and fifty-seven words from Jewish sources which corresponds to the complete Lord's Prayer (which, however, is only a third as long). Such parallelisms should not shock us. The work of a great artist is not to manufacture his paints, but with them to paint a noble picture. So Jesus, using older materials, made his perfect Prayer. On the positive side we may find the originality of the Prayer in

(1) its brevity. Here is no *polylogia*—no holy loquacity, but six short petitions that go arrow-like to the unseen world.

(2) its order. The Prayer puts first things first, the heavenly things before the earthly.

(3) its universality. It is concerned wholly with the needs common to all humanity, so that all men, whatever their class or colour, can make it their own.

The plan of the Prayer is simple. After the Address, or Invocation, come six petitions: three for God's glory, and three for man's needs. First, we are to pray for God's greater glory—the honouring of his name, the coming of his Reign, the doing of his will—then for our human wants: provision, pardon and protection. First, world issues, then human needs; but both, for Jesus, are in the hands of the great Father who at once shapes the course of history and attends to the individual needs of his children.

We name it 'the Lord's Prayer'; and so it is: but because he taught it, not because he prayed it. We cannot conceive of Jesus, who showed no consciousness of sin, praying to be forgiven. He gave the Prayer, as Luke tells us, because the disciples asked for it: it was meant for their use, not his. Did he give it as a formula or as a guide? Probably the latter; yet we do not use the Prayer amiss if we repeat it as we do, so long as we try to pray it with the full force of our heart, avoiding the danger of 'pattered Paternosters'. This Prayer, one of the two things which come to us directly from our Lord (the other is the Lord's Supper) should be the mould and type of all Christian prayer. Understand this prayer, and you understand how a disciple of Christ ought to pray. Do you wish to know whether you can pray for this or that thing in Jesus' name? Then ask yourself: Can it be legitimately covered by the petitions of the Lord's Prayer?

Moreover, its depths cannot be fathomed. A letter of

Thomas Carlyle's, written shortly before he died, tells how the old man, during a sleepless night, set himself to think out the Lord's Prayer, and at every point found himself carried beyond his depth. If a child can understand enough of this Prayer to make it his own, the saint or sage can never exhaust it.

9 *Our Father which art in heaven.* This is the Invocation, or Address. Its first word *our*, like the following '*our* bread' and '*our* debts', reminds us that this is a social prayer. As 'the Bible knows nothing of solitary religion', no man can be a Christian by himself. When we say the prayer we join ourselves with the whole family of God before the throne of grace.

Father is Jesus' characteristic name for God. Only here does he say 'our Father'. Elsewhere it is 'Father' or 'my Father' or 'your Father'. We err if we claim that Jesus was the first to name God 'Father'. Here and there in the Old Testament (e.g. Deut. 32.6) God is invoked as the Father of the nation; and in the Apocrypha (e.g. Ecclus 23.1), as later among the rabbis, we find men beginning to speak of God as the Father of the individual. This hint—this intuition—this budding belief Jesus took up and 'fulfilled'. He gave it a centrality that transformed men's thoughts of God; and he did so because the Father was the supreme reality of his own life. Indeed, he claimed to be the only true mediator of the divine Father to men (Matt. 11.26; Luke 10.22). The title means that God is not a cosmic principle, but a living Person: it connotes authority, goodness, love. If we are to think aright of the divine Father (said Jesus) we must think of human fatherhood at its best, and multiply it by infinity (Matt. 7.11; Luke 11.13). His finest picture of the unseen Father is that limned in the parable of the Prodigal Son. And that Father Jesus revealed in two ways—first, by being so like him that later men came to call him 'the image of God'; and, second, by living a life of such perfect filial trust and obedience that for Christians God became 'the Father of our Lord Jesus Christ'. Everything in prayer turns upon the kind of God we pray to. For the Christian, the word which holds the secret of man's true communion with the unseen is 'Father'—the Father of Jesus, and 'our Father', through him.

Which art in heaven. A Jewish phrase which stresses the separateness of God. Not so much (if the irreverence may be pardoned) God's postal address, as a reminder that if God is Father, he is a holy Father: the Father (as the *Te Deum* says) 'of an infinite majesty' who demands our reverence as well as our love.

Hallowed be thy name. The first petition, striking, at the outset, the note of adoration. To 'hallow' is to treat as holy, to honour, to revere. In the Bible the 'name' means 'the nature'. God's name is his nature as made known to men. God has made himself known to men—has spelt out his great name to them—in nature, in conscience, in his prophets, in his mighty acts in history, above all, in Jesus Christ his only Son. So, in this petition, we pray that men may reverence God in all these ways in which he reveals himself. It is to pray that his revelation of himself may be accepted by all men, and that he may be honoured and revered in conduct and worship, in Church and State, on Sunday and on weekday.

10 *Thy kingdom come.* 'A prayer in which the kingdom is never mentioned,' said one of the rabbis, 'is no true prayer.' Every pious Jew in our Lord's day prayed in the words of the *Kaddish*, 'May his Kingdom be established in your lifetime.'

What does the kingdom of God mean and how does it come? The Kingdom means the 'sovereignty' or 'reign' of God. It signifies not some man-made Utopia but God regnant and redemptive—God breaking decisively into history in judgment and blessing. For the Jew, the Kingdom was the great hope of the future—the God-appointed End to which the whole course of history moved. For centuries, in their misery, they had dreamed of the time when Isaiah's great prophecy (Isa. 52.7ff.) would come true, and there would appear a messenger with the glad, good tidings that God had really begun to reign.

'The time,' said Jesus 'is fulfilled.' (Mark 1.15.) Jesus began his work by declaring that this blessed time had now arrived. In his person, in his ministry and mission, God was acting decisively to visit and redeem his people. The kingdom was here. But it was only a beginning. One day the Reign of God, now small as a mustard-seed, would grow into a great tree, would come 'with power', would cover the earth.

When therefore we pray, 'thy kingdom come', we pray God to complete his great purpose of salvation begun in the life, death and resurrection of Jesus, the coming of the Spirit, the creation of the new Israel, which is the Church. We pray that his sovereignty will be known and acknowledged throughout the world. But the perfect reign of God can never be completely in time, and on this earth. So we pray also that God will at last consummate his Reign, make a final end of all evil, wind up history, and in the bliss of his eternity, 'wipe away all tears' and reward the faith and patience of his saints.

So the Kingdom is, for us, at once, a reality and a hope. If its consummation is still to come, we are already living in the glad reality of the Kingdom, and in the death and resurrection of our Lord the decisive battle has been fought and won.

Thy will be done, as in heaven, so on earth. This petition is not in Luke's version of the prayer. God alone can bring in his Kingdom; but that does not mean that man should sit back with folded arms and wait for the consummation. Man has his part play. It is a pity that all too often we interpret this petition as a pious cry of resignation—of

Christian fatalism—in time of sorrow. 'We have turned,' said William Temple, 'what was meant to be a battle-cry into a wailing litany.' T. W. Manson goes further and gives it a personal reference: 'Thy will be done, and *done by me.*'

But what is God's will? In the light of his revelation in Christ, the answer is not doubtful. God's will is what pleases God. It is health, not disease; purity, not lust; service, not selfishness; giving, not grabbing; love and not hate; the Golden Rule and not the rule of the jungle. In heaven, it is always so; and we pray that earth may become, in this regard, like heaven.

With this clause, the first half of the prayer comes to an end. Having 'asked for the big things', we now turn to pray for man's needs—for his provision, his pardon, and his protection.

11 *Give us this day our daily bread.* If 'man shall not live by bread alone', he needs it for his existence, and he must pray for material provision. This petition teaches our dependence upon God. We do not command the harvest; God gives it. Our daily bread comes from the loving provision of our Father. For

> Back of the loaf is the snowy flour,
>   And back of the flour is the mill,
> And back of the mill is the sun and the shower
>   And the wheat, and the Father's will.

And this, our dependence, we acknowledge whenever we 'say grace'.

Many of the early Fathers took this as a petition for *spiritual*, or sacramental bread. We may confidently reject their exegesis. There is 'a holy materialism' in Christianity, and the primary reference here is certainly to physical bread, bread a man can put his teeth into. It authorizes us to ask God for the necessities of life, what we call 'our bread and butter'. But, as T. T. Lynch reminds us, 'it is a prayer for daily bread and not for daily cake', for the staff of life, and not for luxury. Of course it is not an injunction to idleness: it does not rule out the human effort required to make God's gift our own. 'God feeds the sparrows,' it has been said, 'but he doesn't put the crumbs into their mouths.' And we have the apostolic command that if a man will not work, neither shall he eat (II Thess. 3.10).

But there is a crux in this clause, the meaning of the Greek word *epiousios* which underlies our English word 'daily'. At least three interpretations are possible of this Greek word which is found certainly only here. We may derive it from the Greek word *ousia*, 'subsistence'. 'Give us this day the bread for subsistence.' Or we may derive it from the present participle (feminine) of the Greek verb 'to be' (*ousan*), and translate: 'Give us to-day the bread that pertains to the day.' Or, with many modern scholars, we may derive it from *epiousa*, 'following' (*hemera*, 'day', being understood), and render: 'Give us this day our bread for the *coming* day.' Used in the morning, this petition would ask bread for the day just beginning. Used in the evening, it would pray for to-morrow's bread. It is no objection to this to quote Matt. 6.34: 'Be not anxious for the morrow.' Believing prayer is the opposite of carking care. When we throw the burden upon God by asking for to-morrow's bread, we are dispelling anxiety. Whichever interpretation be preferred, 'the humble believer' with no Greek can rest assured that 'daily' cannot be far wrong, and may even (as Nestlé argues) be right. As a translation it evades all the difficulties, and expresses the thought that was certainly in Jesus' mind.

12 *And forgive us our debts.* Give is followed by forgive. There is another hunger—the hunger of the soul for the forgiveness of the sin that separates it from God. If God is our Father, he is a holy Father who cannot palter with sin. And every one of us is a sinner. 'If we say, We have

no sin, we deceive ourselves, and the truth is not in us'
(I John 1.8). Though Christ has died to redeem us from
our sins, each day we do things—or fail to do things—
which need God's forgiveness.[21]

Such sins Matthew calls 'debts'. Luke has the more
general 'sins'. They are probably variant translations of the
Aramaic word *hoba* used by Jesus. 'Debt' was a Jewish
metaphor for sin of which Jesus made use several times.
(See Matt. 18.23-35 and Luke 7.41-3.) It views sin as an
obligation placed on us by God which we have failed to
meet. The word may stand for everything that we should
be and do towards God, our fellow-men and ourselves.
These things mar the family relationship between the
Father and his children, so that every day we must repent
of them and ask for God's forgiveness.

As we also have forgiven our debtors. But there is a
condition attached to God's forgiveness—a condition which
made Augustine call this 'the terrible petition'—that we
must have forgiven our erring brethren. Not once but many
times Jesus insisted that 'the inward flow of God's forgiveness is impossible without the outward flow of forgiveness
to others'. For God cannot enter the frozen heart of him
who hates. 'Unforgiving, unforgiven' is a law of the spiritual
world over which our Father reigns.

But Matthew's 'as' is open to misunderstanding. It
suggests that God only forgives us to the extent that we
forgive others. Luke's 'for we also forgive' sounds like
an attempt to remove this misinterpretation. And such it
would be. God's forgiveness cannot be a *quid pro quo*
forgiveness. So to interpret it would be to import the
theology of the calculus and the counting-house into the

[24] 'There is the great forgiveness once for all when the man
passes from death to life, to a new relation with God: and there is
the daily forgiveness which renews it in detail and keeps the
channel of grace clean once it has been cut, and prevents it silting
up'—P. T. Forsyth, *God the Holy Father*, 114.

Gospel. Not so have we learned from Jesus to think of God. The divine logic of our Lord runs rather thus: 'If ye then, being evil, know how to forgive, how much more does your heavenly Father.' For

> the love of God is broader
> Than the measures of man's mind.

13 *And bring us not into temptation but deliver us from the evil one*. The sixth and last petition (not two separate petitions, as some have held). Luke has nothing corresponding to the second half of the sentence.

It is a prayer for divine protection in time of spiritual danger. But, right at the start, we come face to face with an old difficulty. 'Bring us not into temptation.' Is Jesus implying that God makes men do evil? The solution lies in a proper understanding of the Greek word *peirasmos*, translated 'temptation'. In the New Testament it can bear two senses—a neutral one, and a bad one. In the neutral sense it means simply 'trial'; in the bad sense, it means 'enticement to evil'. Only the former sense can be in place here. For, as St James says, possibly with a hint at this very difficulty, 'God cannot be tempted by evil, neither tempteth he any man' (James 1.13). Thus, the first half of the petition expresses a natural human shrinking from 'trials', 'times of testing' or what we might call 'moral adventures'. True, God does permit such 'trials', and without them we could not develop moral muscle and backbone. Yet every such trial involves the possibility that we may succumb to the downward pull of evil. So we may paraphrase the whole petition: 'Spare us moral adventures, but if they needs must be, give us strength to come victoriously through them.'

Should we read *evil* (AV) or *the evil one* (RV)? So far as the Greek goes, either may be right. In favour of the RV, it may be said that Jesus believed in a personal prince of evil—a view to which many to-day, impressed by the radical wrongness of human affairs and the cosmic range of evil, are returning. 'The devil,' they would say, 'never did a better stroke of work than when he persuaded men to disbelieve in him.' On the other hand, to render 'bring us not into temptation but deliver us from the devil' leaves no connexion between the two clauses, though the 'but' almost demands one. The AV may, therefore, be right.

So the Prayer ends. In the RV we miss the Doxology which rounds off the Prayer in the AV. But though no part of the true text, this early addition (the substance of it is in the *Didache's* version of the Prayer) is a very happy one; for it serves to end the Prayer as it began, in the thought of the sovereignty and glory of God.[25]

14-15 *On Forgiveness.* M. Cf. Mark 11.25.

14 For if ye forgive men their trespasses,
  Your heavenly Father will also forgive you:
15 But if ye forgive not men their trespasses
  Neither will your heavenly Father forgive you.

Matthew has added these sayings as a sort of codicil to the fifth petition of the Prayer. Cf. Mark 11.25. The meaning is as before: unforgiving, unforgiven. When General Oglethorpe said to John Wesley, 'I never forgive', Wesley replied, 'Then I hope, sir, you never sin'.

16-18 *Fasting.* M.

16 Moreover when ye fast,
  Be not as the hypocrites of a sad countenance,
    for they disfigure their faces that they may be seen of men to fast.
  Verily I say unto you, They have received their reward.
17 But thou, when thou fastest,
  Anoint thy head, and wash thy face,

[25] Jeremias insists that Jesus meant his disciples to end the Prayer with an ascription of glory, but left the formulation of it to themselves. (See *The Expository Times*, Feb. 1960, 142.) If this is so, the Doxology is according to 'the mind of Christ'.

18   that thou be not seen of men to fast, but of thy
         Father which is in secret;
     And thy Father which seeth in secret shall recompense
     thee.

After the 'digression' of 7-15 comes the third illustration of true worship, from fasting.

Fasting was a sign of penitence, and specially pious Jews used to fast on Mondays and Thursdays (Luke 18.12). Centuries before, Isaiah, deploring insincere fasting, had condemned those who 'bowed down their heads like a bulrush, and grovelled in sackcloth and ashes' (Isa. 58.5). But the lesson had gone unlearnt. There were still men who, to impress people with their piety, smeared ashes on their faces and looked lugubrious. (It was said of one rabbi, Joshua Ben Ananiah, that 'all the days of his life his face was black because of fasting'.) Jesus does not condemn fasting; he says that a man with a truly contrite heart will let his fasting be known to God alone. So far as his outward demeanour goes, he might be on his way to a 'party'.

For us Christians, fasting raises the whole matter of personal self-discipline. Would Jesus have condemned it? No, not if this and other passages are any guide. Such discipline (he would have said) is a good thing—if it does not breed spiritual pride and hypocrisy. And he would have added that a lowly spirit does not necessarily mean a long face.

They disfigure their faces. These hypocrites, says Jesus, make their faces disappear' (*aphanizousi*), i.e. either by smearing ashes on them, or by leaving them to disappear under an accumulation of dirt. The bystanders, seeing the holy dirt, exclaim: 'There goes a godly man.' And that, says Jesus, is their reward, the reward they bargain for and all the reward they are ever going to get.

C. ITS OUTWORKINGS

(c) In trust and devotion. 6.19-34.

Having shown how the divine ideal should work itself out in individual and social relations (5.21-48) and in worship (6.1-18), Jesus now shows that it demands an undivided devotion to God and a freedom from worry born of trust in his Providence (6.19-34).

19-21 *True Treasures.* M. Cf. Luke 12.33-24, Q.
(Wording varies much.)

19 Lay not up for yourselves treasures upon earth,
  where moth and rust doth consume,
    and where thieves break through and steal:
20 But lay up for yourselves treasures in heaven,
  where neither moth nor rust doth consume,
    and where thieves do not break through nor steal.
21 For where your treasure is,
  there will your heart be also.

Christ does not mean: 'Exert yourselves to get in heaven the things you treasure here on earth.' He means: 'Learn to delight in the things of heaven—of God. Only these last.' To have 'treasures in heaven' is therefore to be 'rich towards God'; it is to live as he approves, purely, helpfully, lovingly; and it includes all 'those little, nameless unremembered acts of kindness and of love' which are 'the best portion of a good man's life'.

The life here condemned is that pilloried in the parable of the Rich Fool (Luke 12.13-21). 'A man's life consisteth not in the abundance of the things which he possesseth' (Luke 12.15). 'Man's chief end is to glorify God and to enjoy him for ever'; but money tends to distract him from that true end. The root of all evil is not money but *the love of it* (I Tim. 6.10). Jesus does not forbid the possession of it. (His advice to the rich young man was a prescription for a special case.) But, knowing its dangers, he insists that money is a means, and not an end, and that everything turns on our stewardship of it. Money must be used for the highest good, or it becomes a snare. The true Christian attitude is not to despise it, but to evaluate it properly and use it nobly.

19 Nowadays most of us put our wealth in banks, or invest it in stocks and shares. In Christ's day the normal thing was to hide it—in house or field. So the Greek word (*brōsis*) rendered 'rust' which means literally 'eating', may equally well refer to the work of 'the worm'. 'Where moth and worm doth consume.' So too the Greek verb for 'break through' suggests the Oriental burglar who does not smash a window but uses a trowel to pierce the clay walls that separate him from his loot.

21 The reason why a man must decide about treasures. His interests are where his investments are, and they draw his heart like a magnet. If his treasure is God, then his heart, like 'poor Susan's' in the poem, 'will be in heaven', even while he walks the dusty ways of earth. If it is money, it will be, like Scrooge's, in his miser's hoard, absorbing 'all thoughts, all passions, all delights'.

Jesus now illustrates the point with two tiny parables—the Single Eye and the Single Service.

22-24 *The Single Eye and the Single Service.*   Q.   Cf. Luke 11.34f. and 16.13.

22   The lamp of the body is the eye:
     If therefore thine eye be single,
        thy whole body shall be full of light.
23   But if thine eye be evil,
        thy whole body shall be full of darkness.
     If therefore the light that is in thee be darkness,
        how great is that darkness!

24 No man can serve two masters:
>   for either he will hate the one and love the other;
>   or else he will hold to the one, and despise the other.
>   Ye cannot serve God and mammon.

A single eye means a sound eye, as an evil one means a diseased one. The good eye does its job—it sees clearly, without double vision, and a man's whole personality is illumined. The bad eye has the opposite effect. Therefore (and this is the application): keep your spirit's eye clear and undistorted that you may be able to see the way of God's will and do it. But let your vision become distorted —by trying to focus it on both heavenly and earthly goods —and the end will be spiritual blindness.

In the parable of the Single Service Jesus points out the moral dangers of money and demands whole-hearted allegiance to God. He is thinking of money's insidious effect on the soul of its possessor. The pursuit of *mammon* (the Aramaic word for 'gain') disables a man for the true service of God. The saying applies not only to the rich who make money their god, but to the poor who would like to do the same.

24 *Serve.* Better 'be a slave to'. In our modern society a man can serve two masters. The slave could not. The word *hate* means in the Biblical idiom 'love less'. Cf. Deut. 21.15; Gen. 29.31-33.

25-34 *Trust and Tranquillity.* Q. Luke 12.22-31.

25 Therefore I say unto you,
>   Be not anxious for your life, what ye shall eat or what ye shall drink;
>   nor yet for your body, what ye shall put on.
>   Is not the life more than the food,
>   and the body than the raiment?
26 Behold the birds of the heaven,
>   that they sow not, neither do they reap, nor gather into barns;

and your heavenly Father feedeth them.
Are not ye of much more value than they?

27 And which of you by being anxious can add one cubit
   unto his stature?

28 And why are ye anxious concerning raiment?
   Consider the lilies of the field, how they grow;
       they toil not, neither do they spin:

29   yet I say unto you, that even Solomon in all his glory
       was not arrayed like one of these.

30 But if God so clothe the grass of the field, which to-day
   is, and to-morrow is cast into the oven, shall he not much

31 more clothe you, O ye of little faith? Be not therefore
   anxious, saying, What shall we eat, or what shall we

32 drink? or wherewithal shall we be clothed? For after all
   these things do the Gentiles seek; for your heavenly Father

33 knoweth that ye have need of all these things. But seek
   ye first his kingdom and his righteousness; and all these

34 things shall be added unto you. Be not therefore anxious
   for the morrow: for the morrow will be anxious for
   itself. Sufficient unto the day is the evil thereof.

Luke 12.22-31 shows these differences. For 'birds of the heaven' (26) Luke has 'ravens'; for 'toil nor spin' (28), 'spin nor weave'. In 31 Luke added 'be not of doubtful mind'; in 33 Luke does not have 'and his righteousness'; 34 is peculiar to Matthew.

How 'Franciscan' this whole passage is! It is one of many evidences that our Lord was 'country-bred'. But can we, most of us twentieth-century town-dwellers, take it as more than a lovely expression of 'the country faith' in first-century Galilee? Consider what Jesus says: 'To be constantly worrying about food and clothes is to miss the true end of life. The secret of tranquillity, so wonderfully illustrated in bird and flower, is trust in a Father able to supply his children's wants. Your one concern should be God's cause. Leave all else in his hands.'

The sheer simplicity of this faith challenges and perplexes us. 'Into our modern world,' says Johannes Weiss,

'with its hurry and its striving, with its desperate struggle
for existence, this song about freedom from care comes
ringing like a strain from the lost Paradise.'[26] We cannot
help asking: what has it to say to us who are daily en-
grossed in the fight to make ends meet, or must we regretfully dismiss it as another Utopian precept?

Before we do that, let us note one or two things. To
begin with, life in the Galilee of Jesus' day was no economic
idyll. With taxation totalling about 8s. in the £ the men
of Galilee had economic worries hardly less than ours.

Next, common sense should tell us that Jesus is not here
bidding his disciples quit work and wait for God to put
bread in their mouths and clothes on their backs. He knew
(had he not worked as a carpenter?) that human labour is
needed to make God's gifts our own.

Thirdly, what Jesus condemns here is not a wise fore-
thought for the future but nervous anxiety about it. Did
he not elsewhere bid men reckon and count the cost? And
do not the birds, whom he chooses as example, build nests
and exercise prevision?

But the main point to remember is that here, as often,
he is putting his truth in an extreme, almost one-sided,
way. What he is stating is a principle of living. And the
principle is surely this, that, taking reasonable care, we
are to face life trustingly, accepting each day fresh
from God, and leaving the unknown future in his hands.

Who will say that we do not need this teaching? We
who take out insurance policies to cover almost every con-
tingency—we who are so concerned about getting a liveli-
hood that we have forgotten the art of living—do need to
be told to trust God more. True, every now and then
history throws up men who really live as Jesus advises.
Francis of Assisi was one. Another was Edward Wilson of
the Antarctic. ('Look at life carelessly,' he wrote, 'the only
things worth worrying about are in ourselves, not in

[26] Quoted by Montefiore.

externals. . . . It's only real carelessness about one's own will and confidence in God's that can teach one to believe that whatever is, is best.'[27]) The rest of us need the challenge of this Franciscan Christianity—need to be told to put our faith in God and go forward trustingly.

27 An ancient crux. The Greek word translated *stature* is *helikia*. It does have this meaning sometimes, e.g. in Luke 19.3. But it does not give very good sense here: 'Which of you by worrying can add a cubit (eighteen inches) to his stature?' We should have expected something more like 'one inch'. On the other hand, *helikia* in the papyri means, much more commonly, 'age' or 'span of life'. If we so take it here, cubit will be a linear measure of time (like 'hand-breadth' in Ps. 39.5) and we may translate: 'Which of you by worrying can add a cubit to his span of life?' This gives good sense. Worrying won't lengthen our life by the smallest amount. Our times are in God's hands. Let us leave them there.

33 What does *righteousness* mean here? Some take it to mean 'conformity to God's will' and think of that perfectness of character to which Jesus calls us. But its meaning may be soteriological rather than ethical. Certainly the Kingdom of God has that sort of meaning: it denotes God's saving sovereignty: it describes God regnant and redemptive. May not *righteousness* have the same meaning here as fitted the fourth Beatitude, i.e. 'God vindicating the right', 'salvation', almost 'victory'? So we might render: 'Seek ye first his sovereignty and salvation.' Let the disciple make God's victory his chief concern, and all other things can be left for God to provide. 'Ask for the big things' runs a saying of our Lord preserved by Origen, 'and the little shall be added unto you. Ask for the heavenly, and the earthly shall be added unto you.'

[27] *Op. cit.*, 56.

34 This verse is not in Luke. Each day, it says, brings its own bundles of cares, and it is foolish to add to-morrow's worries to to-day's.

C. ITS OUTWORKINGS

(d) In treatment of others. 7.1-12.

This, the last main section of the Sermon, deals with the treatment of others, and is rounded off with the Golden Rule. What follows is in the nature of a final charge and epilogue. Of the twelve verses, 6 and 7-11 must have belonged originally to other contexts. The main theme is contained in 1-5 and 12. The men of the Kingdom are to judge other people gently, remembering their own guilt before God, and to treat them as they would like others to treat them.

1-5 *Judge Not.* Q. Luke 6.37-38, 41-42.

1 Judge not, that ye be not judged.
2 For with what judgment ye judge, ye shall be judged;
  And with what measure ye mete, it shall be measured unto you.
3 And why beholdest thou the mote that is in thy brother's eye, but considerest not the beam that is in thine own
4 eye? Or how wilt thou say to thy brother, Let me cast the mote out of thine eye, and lo, the beam is in thine
5 own eye? Thou hypocrite, cast out first the beam out of thine own eye; and then thou shalt see clearly to cast out the mote out of thy brother's eye.

'Judge not!' At first this sounds like, 'Pull down your law-courts!' So Tolstoy construed it. But it is private, not public judging that our Lord has in mind. This is a warning to 'gently scan your brother man': not because (as Burns says) 'to step aside is human', but because we all stand exposed to the divine judgment, and we must not expect mercy from God if we are not ready to be merciful to our fellows. Christ's men are to eschew the censorious spirit. This does not mean that we are not to rebuke obvious and flagrant wickedness. No, 'dogs are to be called dogs, and swine swine', as Bengel observes. But the disciple must not go about fault-finding and flaw-picking. Rather, looking into his own heart, he will find there more than enough to keep him very humble.

The little parable of the Splinter and the Plank (as Moffatt translates) hammers the point home. Of course, you cannot have a plank in your eye—the thing is grotesquely impossible. But does not the very word 'plank' hint that our own sinfulness before God quite dwarfs our brother's fault?

The rabbis were alive to the perils of censoriousness. 'Remove the burrs from yourself,' said one of them, 'before you remove them from others.' Hillel said: 'Judge not thy neighbour till thou comest into his place.' We are so apt to be blind to our own failings, and intolerant of our own vices in other people. The classic example in the Old Testament is King David, whose anger blazed out against the rich man who had taken the poor man's lamb; and behold, the man was himself. 'Whenever you see a fault in any other man or any other church,' advised Phillips Brooks, 'look for it in yourself or in your own church.'

1 *That ye be not judged.* By God. The reason given in the next verse might suggest that the divine judgment operates on a tit-for-tat basis. But as in the Lord's Prayer, we do wisely to take a larger view of the heavenly justice.

6 *On Discrimination.* M.

6 Give not that which is holy unto the dogs,
      Neither cast your pearls before the swine,
    Lest they trample them under their feet,
      And turn again and rend you.

An isolated saying, doubtless suggested to Matthew by the previous prohibition of judging.

Jesus had called the Kingdom a mystery entrusted to the disciples (Mark 4.11) and likened it to a pearl of great price (Matt. 13.45f.). If we remember that dogs and swine, two typical unclean animals, signify men who cannot appreciate holy things, the meaning is that we must not press the Gospel on those who despise it. Disciples are to be uncritical; but they are not to be undiscriminating in their communication of God's truth. This was a principle of Jesus himself (see Matt. 10.13 and Luke 10.6); and in his own practice he discriminated. (He did not, for example, shout the truth of God's Fatherhood from the house-tops.) It was also the practice of the early Church who did not deliver the Eucharist or the Lord's Prayer to men till they were ready for it. So with ourselves. We are not to shriek the deepest secrets of the Faith at the street-corner, but wait till men show evidence of wanting to know more about them. 'Let the Church,' comments Bishop Gore, 'show her compassion and goodness and geniality to all men, but not press upon them the mysteries of God until, under her discipline and teaching, they begin to show some disposition to receive them.'[28]

7-11 *On Prayer.* Q. Luke 11.9-13.

7   Ask, and it shall be given you;
         Seek, and ye shall find;
             Knock, and it shall be opened unto you.
8   For everyone that asketh receiveth;
         And he that seeketh findeth;
             And to him that knocketh it shall be opened.
9   Or what man is there of you who, if his son shall ask
         him for a loaf, will give him a stone?
10   Or, if he shall ask for a fish, will give him a serpent?

[28] *The Sermon on the Mount*, 164.

11 If ye then, being evil, know how to give good gifts unto
       your children,
    How much more shall your Father which is in heaven
       give good things to them that ask him?

This passage on prayer stands in no topical relation with
its context. In Luke it fittingly follows the Lord's Prayer
and the parable of the Friend at Midnight. Luke has 'egg'
and 'scorpion' for Matthew's 'loaf' and 'stone', and 'Holy
Spirit' for Matthew's 'good things'. In view of Luke's stress
on the Spirit, Matthew's version must be preferred in the
last case.

Using the three metaphors of asking, seeking and knock-
ing, Jesus promises his disciples that God will answer their
prayers, if only they persevere. If human parents, bad as
they are, give their children what they need, how much
more will the good Father above! The promise is made
absolutely. It sounds like a spiritual blank cheque authoriz-
ing us to draw as we will on the resources of Omnipotence.
But, of course, we must supply the necessary conditions
from Christ's other teaching; as, for example, that our
requests must accord with the spirit and design of the
Lord's Prayer, and that we must say, as Jesus himself said,
'Not what I will, but what thou wilt.'

God, says Jesus, will give *good things*. What does he
mean? The Lord's Prayer will guide us. The things that
belong to God's Kingdom and his children's needs. Not
fame or wealth or unclouded happiness—Jesus never promises such things—but daily bread, daily forgiveness, daily
light and leading and protection.

9f. Jesus must have in mind a fish resembling a snake,
and a round stone like a loaf.

11 The argument is: 'No human father—and the best of
them are far from perfect—would play a scurvy trick like
this on his child. How much less then the holy father

above!' If only Christian theology had always been regulated by some such saying of Jesus as this, we might have been spared not only shocking pictures of hell but sugary conceptions of heaven.

If ye then being evil. How quietly Jesus assumes man's fallen state—that there is an ugly twist in us all! He never despairs of human nature, but he knows too well 'what is in man' to indulge in any sky-blue doctrines of man's natural goodness.

12 *The Golden Rule.* Q. Luke 6.31.

12 All things therefore whatsoever ye would that men should do unto you, even so do ye also unto them: for this is the law and the prophets.

The Golden Rule serves as capstone to the Sermon. The two versions of it are probably variant translations of the Aramaic. Since Matthew likes to add the word 'all' or 'all things', Luke's briefer version is probably more original.

Parallels to the Rule can be found in both Jewish and Gentile sources, as though to prove that God had not left men without knowledge of the highest morality before the coming of Christ. In Tob. 4.15 we read: 'What thou hatest do to no man.' Hillel said: 'What is hateful to thee do not to anyone else.' The Stoics had a maxim: 'Do not to another what you do not wish to happen to yourself.' In Confucius we find: 'Do not to others what you would not wish done to yourself.'

All these are negative, and in the negative form the conduct called for need not rise much above a calculating prudence anxious to avoid trouble. Christ's Rule is positive. He insists not merely that we do not do evil to another but that we do him active good. Moreover, it is the principle behind the saying that matters. (Some take it too literally, and behave as if everyone must agree with them in what they like or dislike.) We are to treat others with the same considerateness we would like them to show to us. And this principle is capable of extension to cover all sorts of circumstances. We are to ask ourselves, 'How would I like the other fellow to treat me?' and then translate the resulting insight into loving treatment of our fellow man. Kant was never more Christian than when he wrote: 'So act as to treat humanity, whether in your own person or that of another, in every case as an end, not as a means only.'

Elsewhere Jesus had summed up man's duty to the two worlds—the seen and the unseen—in the great twin-command (Mark 12.29-31): 'Love God—and love your neighbour as yourself.' To this he adds the Golden Rule, 'Do as you would be done by'—brief, portable, rememberable. While Israel was 'making a dark mystery out of God's law' and driving earnest souls like Saul of Tarsus to despair, Jesus bade men find in the Command and the Rule the heart of religion and ethics. For him, they superseded all other rules and regulations; and they remain for us a simple and sufficient guide to the good life.

For this is the law and the prophets. Not in Luke. The words remind us of Matt. 5.17 and Rom. 13.9, and seem to mean: 'This is the principle in which the true spirit of the Old Testament culminates.' (Gore.)

D. THE WAY OF LIFE

Profession and Practice. 7.13-27.

The Sermon proper is at an end. It remains only for Jesus in the parable of the Two Ways, the Two Trees and the Two Houses to challenge his disciples to strenuous living, to a profession that will issue in the doing of God's will, and to a building of their lives on the divine pattern he has given them.

13-14   *The Two Ways.*   M.   Cf. Luke 13.23f.

13   Enter ye in by the narrow gate:
    for wide is the gate, and broad is the way that leadeth
       to destruction,
    and many be they that enter in thereby.
14   For narrow is the gate,
    and straitened the way that leadeth unto life,
       and few be they that find it.

Using the old figure of the Two Ways (Ps. 1; Jer. 21.8;
etc.) Jesus challenges men to decide for or against the
Kingdom.

Two ways (he says) open out before them: the easy way
of self-indulgence, the hard way of self-denial. There are
always many willing to walk the first way, few the second.
But these ways lead to quite different destinations: one to
destruction (which is separation from God), the other to
life (which is being in the presence of God).

The *narrow gate* probably denotes entrance into the
Kingdom, and the *straitened way* the life to be lived after
entrance. It is a reminder not only 'how very hard it is
to be a Christian' but also that, as an old Scotsman put it,
the Christian life is 'a sair warstle to the very end'.

And few be they that find it. Does this suggest that in
Christ's view the 'many' are doomed to perdition? Then
let us beware of deducing from a single saying a whole
eschatology which will enable us to estimate the populations
of heaven and hell, and let us remember that it is this same
Jesus who says that it is the purpose of his dying to ransom
'the many' (Mark 10.45). Moreover, in the Lucan passage
likest this (Luke 13.23f.) Jesus refuses a direct answer to
the question, 'Are those on the way to salvation few?'
'Take heed,' he says in effect, 'you cannot saunter into the
Kingdom. Leave the fate of the many to God.'

15-23 *The Two Trees.* Q + M. Cf. Luke 6.43f., 46; 13.26f.

15 Beware of false prophets, which come to you in sheep's
16 clothing, but inwardly are ravening wolves. By their fruits ye shall know them. Do men gather grapes of thorns, or figs of thistles?

17 Even so every good tree bringeth forth good fruit,
   But the corrupt tree bringeth forth evil fruit,
18 A good tree cannot bring forth evil fruit,
   Neither can a corrupt tree bring forth good fruit.
19 Every tree that bringeth not forth good fruit is hewn
20 down, and cast into the fire. Therefore by their fruits ye shall know them.

21 Not every one that saith unto me, Lord, Lord, shall enter into the kingdom of heaven; but he that doeth the
22 will of my Father which is in heaven. Many will say to me in that day, Lord, Lord, did we not prophesy by thy name, and by thy name cast out devils, and by thy name
23 do many mighty works? And then will I profess unto them, I never knew you: depart from me ye that work iniquity.

This section, which we have called 'the Two Trees', is a mixture of sayings from M and Q. (Vss. 16-18 are fairly close to Luke 6.43-44, and the thought of vss. 21-23 resembles that of Luke 6.46 and 13.26-27.)

Concerned for the future of the New Israel (of which the disciples are the nucleus) Jesus foresees dangers and issues warnings.

'I warn you,' he says, 'against false teachers,[29] whose looks may so easily mislead. Personal character is the thing to look out for. The test of a tree is the quality of the fruit it bears: so it is with men. Pious professions alone will never save a man. On Judgment Day many who proudly claim to have done wonderful things in my name may be shocked to find themselves disowned.'

[29] Vs. 15 may reflect the rise of false leaders in the early Church.

'Character is the one thing needful' seems to be the main thought. A good character, for Jesus, is the product of a pure heart. As like produces like—you cannot expect to find Cox's Orange on a crab-apple tree—so real goodness is the fruit of a heart cleansed by God's grace. This was one of the great Reformation insights, admirably phrased by Luther: 'It is not good works which make a good man, but a good man who does good works.' So, as Jesus puts it in another place (Matt. 12.33), first, make the tree good'.

'*Not every one that saith unto me Lord, Lord. . . .*' How impatient Jesus is of pious professions that do not issue in practice! St Luke's version of the saying (which is probably more original) is even blunter: 'Why do ye call me Lord, Lord, and do not the things which I say?' (Luke 6.46).

Notice, too, what a tremendous personal claim is implicit in the last two verses of the section. The Peasant-Preacher of the Sermon implies that one day he will judge the world, that he will be the Arbiter of every man's destiny. In that day more than a mere naming of Christ's name will be required. 'Lord, Lord, have we not prophesied in thy name?' is a warning to all of us who preach or write; for, its modern equivalent, as Bengel puts it, might be: 'We have written commentaries on the Old and New Testaments. We have preached splendid sermons.'

16 Luke has 'figs of thorns' and grapes of a bramble bush'. Thorns and thistles are typical weeds.

17 The Greek word *sapros* rendered *corrupt* probably means 'bad' in the sense of being unfit for eating.

19 This is a saying of the Baptist (see Matt. 3.10) which has somehow slipped in here.

23 *I never knew you* seems to mean, in rabbinical idiom,

'I don't want any dealings with you'. The final phrase is from Ps. 6.9. (For Matthew's *iniquity* Luke has *un-righteousness*.)

24-27   *The Two Houses.*   Q.   Luke 6.47-49.

24   Every one therefore which heareth these words of mine
　　　　and doeth them
　　　Shall be likened unto a wise man which built his house
　　　　upon the rock:
25   And the rain descended,
　　　And the floods came,
　　　And the winds blew,
　　　And beat upon that house,
　　　And it fell not;
　　　For it was founded upon the rock.
26   And everyone that heareth these words of mine, and doeth
　　　　them not,
　　　Shall be likened unto a foolish man, which built his house
　　　　upon the sand:
27   And the rain descended,
　　　And the floods came
　　　And the winds blew,
　　　And smote upon that house;
　　　And it fell:
　　　And great was the fall of it.

The Parable of the Two Houses closes the Sermon most impressively and 'strikes for a verdict', as every true sermon should.

If we compare St Matthew's version of it with St Luke's, we shall find that in almost every respect—literary structure, dramatic quality, and local colour—the First Evangelist's is to be preferred.

The question poses itself: Is the Sermon on the Mount a collection of sweet, impossible precepts, which, while we admire them, we must regretfully reject as utterly beyond our power of practice? This parable supplies the answer. However far we come short of the Sermon's Design for

Life, Jesus clearly means his disciples to fashion their lives on the basis of the principles he has laid down in it.

The meaning of the parable is plain. The rock-built house stands for hearing *and* doing Christ's words; the house built on sand for hearing them only; and the storm is any time of severe testing or tribulation in the life of the individual or the Church. In such a time, the secret of security will be a character built on the word and person of Jesus.

Once again, we cannot miss the tremendous claim implicit in the parable. 'The Carpenter of Nazareth stands before the whole race of mankind, and tells them that he has laid down principles of conduct which they will neglect at their peril.' His Design for Life is the only one which will last. Only One who was conscious that his will was completely synonymous with the Divine Will could so speak. We do not wonder that, as Matthew tells us in the closing verses of the chapter, 'the multitudes were astonished at his teaching'. After nineteen hundred years we are astonished too.

Part Three

THE MEANING OF
THE SERMON

IV

THE SERMON AND
ITS INTERPRETERS

W E might suppose that such an apparently simple document as the Sermon on the Mount, while permitting dis-
agreement on details of exegesis, would hardly allow much
differences of opinion on its main meaning. In fact, the
views taken of the Sermon have been almost as varied as
the portraits men have drawn of the Preacher himself.

Those who wish to know how the Sermon was interpreted
in the early Church and at the Reformation may be referred
to Harvey McArthur's excellent *Understanding the Sermon
on the Mount*. In this chapter we propose to review some
modern interpretations.

I

Let us start with Tolstoy, the great Russian novelist
whose interpretation of Jesus' moral teaching deeply influ-
enced Gandhi. It was in the Sermon on the Mount that
Tolstoy found the blueprint for his new society when he
turned social reformer later in his life. The Sermon, he
held, is the new law of Jesus, abrogating the old law of
Moses, and its kernel is to be found in Matt. 5.21-48 with
its imperatives to be taken quite literally and applied absolutely and universally. 'Swear not at all,' said Jesus. This
means, said Tolstoy, an end to all oaths, even in law-courts.
'Resist not evil,' said Jesus. This means: scrap the police-
force and all resisters of evil. (It can also mean, and may
well mean in practice: let thugs and gangsters have their

own sweet way. But Tolstoy apparently did not bother about that.) He saw in the Sermon the new moral law to be carried out *au pied de la lettre* by all Christians. Let them only do this, and we should have the Kingdom of God on earth.

We may well quarrel with Tolstoy's view of the Sermon as a new Law—holding Jesus to be no legislator—as we must criticize his resolve to take everything quite literally Let this at least be said in his favour. He was a witness to the truth that Jesus gave his commandments in order that they should be obeyed.

We may call his view an absolutist or perfectionist ethic.

II

For Tolstoy the Kingdom of God was some sort of terrestrial Utopia. How differently it appeared at the start of this century to Albert Schweitzer of Alsace! For him the Kingdom was to be understood only in terms of pre-Christian Messianism and apocalyptic. So far from being a man-made paradise, it meant the catastrophic irruption of God into history, bringing with it the end of the world and the Day of Judgment. The imminence of this Kingdom was the burden of all Jesus' preaching.

What then are we to make of his ethical teaching in general and the Sermon in particular? It was, answered Schweitzer, 'an ethic of the interval' (*Interimsethik*). Just as in war-time laws are hurriedly promulgated to cover the time of crisis, so Jesus' ethic was an emergency ethic for his disciples' use during the brief interval—a few months, at most a year or two—between his preaching and the cataclysmic coming of the Kingdom of God. But since in fact the world did not suddenly end in AD 30, the ethical teaching of Jesus can have little obvious relevance for Christians in the twentieth century. (Let us add that Schweitzer's own career since then—despite some recent attempts to disparage him—has been a glorious refutation of what seems the logic of his theory.)

Schweitzer was right in saying that the ethic of Jesus was an eschatological ethic, i.e. that it arises out of his preaching of an eschatological Kingdom of God. The trouble was that Schweitzer used his Gospel sources uncritically and turned a Nelson eye on all those well-attested sayings of Jesus which declare the Reign of God to be already present in Jesus and his mission. The other main criticism to be made of him is that the Sermon on the Mount does not ring with warnings that the end of the world is imminent. When Jesus speaks about marriage or forgiveness or love of enemies, he does not reinforce his words with the warning that 'the hammer of the world's clock stands ready to strike'. He bids his disciples be 'perfect', not because 'the time is shortened', but because God their Father is 'perfect'. He warns them not to lay up treasures on earth, not because the Last Trumpet may sound at any moment, but because 'where your treasure is, there will your heart be also'.

Yet, in a sense, Jesus' ethic is 'an ethic of the interval', since it is a pattern for Christian living in the interval between the coming of God's Kingdom and the final consummation when God will complete the saving work he began in Christ.

III

At the end of the last century when the young Schweitzer was deep in his study of eschatology, a very different view of Jesus and his teaching was being taken by Wilhelm Herrmann of Marburg, the 'unforgettable teacher' of Barth and many others. If Schweitzer saw the Story of Jesus against the background of Jewish apocalyptic, Herrmann found in him 'a revelation of the Living to the living' and saw in the Sermon a *Gesinnungsethik,* an ethic of disposition, or frame-of-mind.

The worst of all mistakes, he said, was to regard Jesus' commandments in the Sermon as laws to be fulfilled in every case. If Jesus had really meant them so, he would have been worse than the Scribes and Pharisees whom he charged with laying on the people intolerable burdens (Matt. 23.4). In fact, Jesus was no legalist. What he sought was his followers' spiritual freedom and all the moral power that comes with it. He was far more concerned with what men should *be* than with what they should *do*. Accordingly we should see in the precepts of the Sermon illustrations of a new set of the mind and will, i.e. of the disposition based on the consciousness that God the Father is the supreme reality and love the highest good.

Unlike Schweitzer, Herrmann held Jesus' teaching to be valid for his followers today; and he has been accused of unduly modernizing it. Yet his interpretation has some clear merits. It lifts the Sermon out of all Jewish legalism; it strongly stresses (as Jesus did) the importance of men's intentions before God; and in its insistence on the primacy of love it is faithful to One who summed up the Law in the twin command of love to God and love to man. Its weakness is the antithesis it sets up between frame of mind and actual deed. No one can read the Sermon without realizing that Jesus took the intention for the act and consistently demanded obedience in actual deed. 'Whosoever hears these words of mine and does them. . . . Why do you call me Lord, Lord, and do not the things which I say?'

IV

A wide gulf separates Herrmann's view of the Sermon from the next one which finds in it an ethic of repentance. Common among Lutherans, it has a modern representative in Gerhard Kittel, the original editor of the famous *Theological Word Book of the New Testament*.

Some have called it 'the Pauline view' because it sees the Sermon in the same way as Paul saw the Law. According to the apostle, the Law awakens the consciousness of sin and by revealing to man his moral impotence opens his eyes to the wonder of God's mercy in the Cross.

So it is with the Sermon. Never intended as practical legislation, its purpose was to lay bare the moral straits of man. As one of Robert Frost's characters puts it,

> The Sermon on the Mount
> Is just a frame-up to insure the failure
> Of all of us, so all of us will be
> Thrown prostrate at the Mercy Seat for mercy.

Seen thus, the Sermon becomes a terrifying summons to repentance. Its moral demands can never be fulfilled, and Jesus never meant them to be. Their true purpose was to bring men to their knees in penitence.

But this is only half the story. As a correlate to the Sermon on the Mount comes the Cross on the Hill. The Sermon prepares man to receive the Gospel of God's forgiving grace in Christ crucified. It leads him straight to the foot of the Cross where God showed his mercy to sinners (Rom. 3.25 and 5.8).

This view, then, fully recognizes the rigour of Christ's demands, but it proposes a theological way-out of the difficulties. No serious Christian will deny that the Sermon, by its revelation of the pure will of God, exposes us as sinners who come far short of the glory of God. But there is not a hint in the Sermon itself, or in the rest of the Gospels, that Jesus meant his moral demands to be the propaedeutic to a Gospel for sinners.

This solution of the problem illustrates what happens when one interprets Jesus by Paul, and not Paul by Jesus. It is Paulinizing *exegesis*—and therefore *eisegesis*.

v

Jesus invited all who laboured under the burdens of the Jewish Law to come to himself if they would find 'relief' and the secret of an obedience that was not imposed but inspired. Was then the Sermon really an ethic of grace rather than of law—or, more accurately, of the response to grace?

This is the view of Joachim Jeremias and many other modern scholars, and of the various interpretations we have reviewed it seems to us the truest and the best. Let us summarize it.

The Sermon as it lies before us now in Matthew represents the design for Christian living which the apostolic Church gave its catechumens—that is, it was preceded by the preaching of the Gospel and conversion. But what is true of the Sermon as a whole is true also of the separate sayings which make it up. Originally they were all preceded by something else—the proclamation of the glad good news of God's inbreaking Reign and the new relationship with God which it made possible. Take an analogy from Greek grammar. In a conditional sentence you have two parts—the *protasis* or 'if' part, and the *apodosis* or 'then' part, indicating what follows from the first. All the commands of the Sermon are *apodoses* which cannot be understood without the great *Protasis* of the Galilean Gospel, that God had broken redeemingly into history and inaugurated his New Order of grace.

If then in the Sermon Jesus says to his disciples, 'You must forgive' (Matt. 6.15), it is because they have already had the glad assurance 'Your sins are forgiven'. If he says, 'You are the light of the world' (Matt. 5.14), it is implied that they already have found in him 'the light of the world' (John 8.12). If he bids them live like sons of God, it is because they already know themselves to be children of Abba, Father. If he calls them to 'love their enemies' (Matt. 5.44), behind his command lies the dynamic of the boundless grace of God. In every instance, the gift of God—his grace—precedes the demand. It is a case of 'Freely you have received, freely give'.

If this be so, the Sermon is not really law but Gospel. Law makes man rely on his own strength and challenges him to do his utmost. But Gospel confronts man with the gift of God and challenges him to make God's gift the basis of his life. This, if we will hear him aright, is what Jesus is doing in the Sermon. The Sermon outlines the response of the men of the Kingdom to the experienced grace of God. We may call it an ethic of appropriation which illustrates, often picturesquely and hyperbolically, the ways in which men enter ever more fully into the experience of grace.

We have argued that the Sermon is best interpreted as an ethic of grace. But since 'grace' can be a highly dangerous word, let us end our survey on a note of warning.

Human nature being what it is, men are always tempted to cheapen grace—to rest comfortably in the belief that 'grace is all' and to forget the costly obedience it ought to involve. We are wont to say that at the Reformation Luther rediscovered the true doctrine of God's grace when it was in grave danger of being smothered beneath a specious doctrine of salvation by works. But all too often this precious truth has been construed as a dispensation from obedience to the commands of Jesus. This is a fatal error: true grace is a costly thing, because it means that we must take ever more seriously Christ's call to discipleship.

This is the thesis of one of the most remarkable expositions of the Sermon in our time—Dietrich Bonhoeffer's *Cost of Discipleship*. He too holds that the Christian ethic is one of grace: but it is costly grace, never cheap grace. 'The word of cheap grace,' he says, 'has been the ruin of more Christians than any commandment of works.' Only grace that issues in a serious following in the way of Jesus is worthy of the name. The Sermon give us the meaning and the content of that discipleship. And there must be no toning down of the demands that Jesus makes in it. Obedience is the one thing needful. 'You can only learn obedience by obeying,' he says, 'It is no use asking questions, for it is only through obedience that you come to learn the truth.'

So in this classic of spiritual devotion Bonhoeffer expounds the meaning of the discipleship to which Jesus calls. As an exegesis of the Sermon, Bonhoeffer's book may be faulted at this point and that, as he sometimes seems to twist texts to suit a preconceived theological formula. But his abiding merit is his insistence on a single-minded discipleship to Jesus as the corollary of grace.

It was said of an ancient philosopher, 'He says the finest things—if only he had the right to say them.' Bonhoeffer had the right, for in his steadfast devotion to Christ he was executed by the S.S. Black Guards in April 1945. And Bonhoeffer, 'being dead, yet speaketh', calling all Christians who have experienced God's grace to take ever more seriously the high obligations of discipleship.

V

THE SERMON
AND THE GOSPEL

W H A T place has the Sermon on the Mount in that revelation of God and his gracious purpose for men which is the
central theme of the New Testament?

Mahatma Gandhi once said: 'The message of Jesus
is contained in the Sermon on the Mount, unadulterated
and taken as a whole.'[1] Many people much less eminent
than he are of the same opinion. It is one of the popular
heresies of our time that the Sermon is the sum of the
Gospel—the essence of Christianity. (The heresy is about
a hundred years old, and is a by-product of the Liberal
scholarship which found the kernel of New Testament
Christianity in Jesus' teaching about the Fatherhood of
God, the brotherhood of man, and the law of love.) When
our popular press, turning pious for the nonce, holds up
Christianity as the sovereign cure for the world's ills, what
they have in mind is not Christian doctrine but what is
vaguely known as 'the Christian Ethic'. And if we ask what
is meant, the odds are that the reply will be in five words,
'The Sermon on the Mount'. This (they imply) is the
essence of the Gospel, and all else is the mystification of
the professional theologian.

Though no reputable New Testament scholar any longer
believes this, the notion lives on in the popular mind and
needs to be refuted.

[1] C. F. Andrews, *Mahatma Gandhi's Ideas*, 93.

One way of doing it is to ask the question, What did the earliest Christians mean by the Gospel?

It was certainly not any such ethical manifesto as the Sermon on the Mount. 'To the Apostles,' said Sir William Robertson Nicoll, 'the insistence on the Sermon on the Mount at the sum of Christianity would have appeared a relapse into hopeless paganism.' Doubtless this goes too far—is too trenchantly stated—but it contains truth.

When St Paul reminded the Christians of Corinth concerning the fundamentals of the apostolic Gospel, he did not summarize them thus:

Blessed are the poor in spirit, the meek, the mourners. Ye are the salt of the earth. Resist not evil. Love your enemies. Be not anxious for the morrow. Do to others as you would have them do to you.

What he wrote was:

I delivered unto you first of all that which also I received, how that Christ died for our sins according to the scriptures; and that he was buried; and that he hath been raised on the third day according to the scriptures; and that he appeared to Cephas; then to the twelve. . . . (I Cor. 15.3ff.)

To put it briefly, the Gospel with which the apostles went forth to 'turn the whole world upside down' was not good advice, but good news. It told of a divine act rather than a divine demand. It was *kerygma*—the proclamation of how God, in fulfilment of his ancient promises, had broken into history in the life, death and resurrection of Jesus his Messiah, for us men and for our salvation.

To be sure, this proclamation involved what we should call ethical issues and consequences. The Good News of God's intervention in Christ carried with it, as corollary, a summons to those who accepted it to behave in a new way; and the moral teaching of him who was the centre of this Good News obviously gave guidance in this direction. To this point was shall come back. The point we are making now is that for the earliest Christians the central thing was the Cross on the Hill and the Empty Tomb, not the Sermon on the Mount. In the mission and ministry of Jesus the Messiah, in his mighty works, his Cross, his victory over the grave, and in the gift of the Spirit, God had decisively manifested his Kingdom, and men must know about it, and accept this news as true, if they were to be saved. This, not the Sermon on the Mount, was the heart of the earliest Gospel.

The other way to settle the matter is to read the Sermon on the Mount itself and think out just what it involves. Some people imagine that the Sermon is a collection of plain, practical rules for right living which mankind at large could easily carry out, if only it had a mind to. 'Give us less theology,' is their cry, 'and more of the Sermon on the Mount.' (It is worth observing that the supposedly untheological Sermon contains a good deal more theology than they imagine, though it does not lie on the surface.) Like the sons of Zebedee, they do not quite know what they are asking. Let any man gravely consider what is implied in Christ's exposition of 'the higher righteousness' (Matt. 5.21-48)—no anger, no lustful thought, no swearing, no resistance to evil, etc.—and then let him ask himself what good news—what Gospel is there. If God means that, in order to be saved, we must completely fulfil all these demands, then we are doomed to be damned. If the old Law of Israel killed when it was meant to make alive, this new Law of Jesus—if it is a law in that sense—kills a hundred times more effectively. Taken by itself, this Sermon (said Scott Holland[2]) which some lightly suppose to be the heart of the Gospel, is in reality a sentence of doom; for it shows how far we all come short of the glory of God revealed in Jesus Christ.

What then is the place of the Sermon in the Christian scheme of things?

[2] *Creed and Character*, 238f.

We said a moment ago that the apostolic Gospel involved ethical consequences. Let us put it this way. Since the Kingdom (or Reign) of God had come in Christ, then obviously believers in him were committed to live in 'a Kingdom way'. Or, as St John would have put it, the 'Gospel' implied also the 'Commandment'.

Now the New Testament makes it clear that the early Church's message always followed some such pattern. It had two aspects—one theological, the other ethical: (i) the Gospel which the apostles preached; and (ii) the Commandment, growing out of the Gospel, which they taught to those who accepted the Gospel. The Gospel was a declaration of what God, in his grace, had done for men through Christ; the Commandment was a statement of what God required from men who had become the objects of his gracious action.

You may observe this pattern in a typical Pauline epistle. After beginning his letter with some aspect of the Gospel, Paul is wont to end it with a 'practical' section setting forth the moral standards required of believers. First, some statement of the grace of God in Christ, then an explication of the Christian conduct expected from the recipients of that grace. But in this Paul was only doing what his Lord had done before him. Jesus not only proclaimed that the Kingdom of God had come with himself and his work; he also set before his disciples the moral ideal of that Kingdom. The sayings of Jesus gathered together in the Sermon on the Mount represent not Jesus' 'Gospel' but his 'Commandment'. They are his design for living in the Kingdom, given to his disciples during many hours of teaching in Galilee before he went up to Jerusalem to finish his work. There followed the mighty acts—the Cross, the Resurrection, the gift of the Spirit—by which the Kingdom came 'with power'. And after Pentecost, when the young Church was faced with the problem of instructing converts in the new way of life required of them, they turned, naturally enough, to Christ's own design for living as it survived in the memories of those who had been his original disciples.

Nineteen centuries have gone past. Yet for us who worship the same living Lord the moral ideal remains the same. It is the ideal adumbrated in the Sermon on the Mount.

VI

THE SERMON AND THE
ETHIC OF JESUS

CAN we really talk about 'the ethic of Jesus'? It is true that we have a number of books with such titles as *The Ethic of Jesus, The Moral Teaching of Jesus*, etc., and many treatises on *Christian Ethics*, all of which begin with some account of our Lord's moral teaching. But is this a proper use of language? Dean Inge[1] has said: 'The Synoptic Gospels give us a standard of values and an example—these and little more.' There is truth in this. Jesus did not appear before men primarily in the role of an ethical teacher—a Galilean Socrates telling men that 'virtue is knowledge and vice is ignorance'. 'If Christianity was morals,' said Blake, 'then Socrates was the Saviour.' Further, we look in vain in the Gospels for anything like a *system* of ethics. Even the Sermon on the Mount which is the nearest approach to it, represents, as we have seen, the gathering together by Matthew of many fragments of teaching—many *obiter docta* of Jesus. And yet, since ethics is the science of conduct, and Jesus did undoubtedly have a great deal to say about conduct; and since, moreover, there is a deep underlying unity—a wholeness springing from the one unique personality who uttered the sayings—in what our Lord has to say about moral problems, we may legitimately speak about a Gospel ethic or an ethic of Jesus.

In this final chapter, therefore, gathering up the judgments and conclusions to which we have been tending in

[1] *Christian Ethics and Modern Problems*, 41.

the previous ones and in the exegesis of the Sermon itself, we propose to put forward four theses about the ethic of Jesus and to defend them:

1. It is a *religious* ethic.
2. It is a *disciples'* ethic.
3. It is a *prophetic* ethic—not a new law.
4. It is an *unattainable* ethic which, as Christians, we must nevertheless try to attain.

I

Our first thesis, that the ethic of Jesus is a religious ethic, few will dispute. By a religious ethic we mean that it is a morality based on religious premises.

Not all ethical systems are religious. Philosophical moralists generally start, as Bishop Butler did, from the constitution of man's nature and the obligations laid on him as a social being. Likewise, Utilitarians like Bentham begin from the necessity of producing the greatest happiness for the greatest number. But Biblical ethics always presuppose Biblical religion: they are based upon belief in the living God. We tend to divide up religion and ethics into two separate compartments. The Bible never does this. Rather, Biblical ethics grow out of Biblical religion—they are its practical expression, its flowering in life and conduct. Consider the preface to the Decalogue: 'I am the Lord thy God which brought thee out of the land of Egypt. . . . Therefore, thou shalt. . . .' So it is with the ethic of Jesus. Its postulate is faith in God—faith in the Father whom he revealed, as the sanctions which he invokes are always religious sanctions: rewards and punishments, the imitation of God, the promotion of his greater glory, etc.

Yet it is not enough to say that Jesus' ethic is religious in this general way. His ethic presupposes not only belief in the one true and living God but the whole Gospel of the Reign of God which was the central theme of his preaching. To understand Jesus' ethic aright, we have to remember what he taught about the Kingdom of God and its coming. For him, the Kingdom of God was the sovereignty of God in action—God intervening decisively in history to visit and redeem his people—and the heart of his Good News was the announcement that that glad era for whose advent prophets and kings had yearned, was now at last becoming a reality. The Reign of God had begun— had begun with himself and his ministry.

So we have to do with both a divine indicative and a divine imperative. But the imperative is founded on the indicative. The divine indicative may be expressed like this: 'God has manifested his Kingdom—his saving Rule—in Christ.' The imperative will then run something like this: 'Therefore let all who accept the Rule of God live in a new way—the Kingdom way.' What that new way should be, the Sermon on the Mount makes plain. It is a design for life in the Kingdom of God.

We may sum up the first point by saying that the ethic of Jesus is a religious ethic, and that the 'good advice' of the Sermon on the Mount is rooted and grounded in the 'Good News' of the Kingdom of God.

II

The ethic of Jesus, of which the Sermon is a summary, is essentially a disciples' ethic. It was given as a way of life for the men of the Kingdom, not for mankind at large.

This is really a corollary of our first conclusion, but it is important enough to deserve separate emphasis. Those who from time to time, amid the world's evil and chaos, cry out 'Give us the Sermon on the Mount, and all will be well', apparently assume that the ethic of the Sermon is a morality for all men. Diametrically opposed to them are those who tell us that 'the Sermon was an ordination charge to the Twelve'. The latter are undoubtedly nearer the truth. The

Sermon is fundamentally disciple-teaching, but we need not restrict the term 'disciple' to the chosen Twelve. Besides the dozen men appointed by Christ to be the nucleus of the new Israel (how significant the number twelve is!) there were clearly others—a sort of outer circle over against the inner one—attached to Christ in a looser sort of discipleship. To this whole body of followers we may suppose the bulk of the Sermon to have been delivered.

In the opening verses of Matt. 5 we are told that the disciples formed the audience for the Sermon. A study of the Sermon itself confirms this. The Beatitudes—especially in the second-person-plural form found in Luke ('Blessed are ye poor,' etc.)—are clearly addressed not to all and sundry but to certain 'committed' men. The following parables of the Salt and the Light point in the same direction. The so-called Lord's Prayer is, as we have seen, a disciples' prayer. 'Lord, teach us to pray, as John also taught his disciples.' And sayings like 'No man can serve two masters', 'Seek ye first the kingdom', 'Give not that which is holy unto the dogs', along with the concluding parable are obviously addressed to men prepared, at any rate, to make the venture of discipleship.

There is little need, however, to elaborate the point, for our best writers on the Sermon are agreed about it, though they may phrase it differently. 'Spoken not to the world but to the Church,' says Gore.[2] 'Given to the new Israel,' comments T. W. Manson.[3] Montefiore[4] sums up: 'Ripe teaching for ripe disciples.'

The point must be borne in mind when we are considering the questions of the relevance and the practicability of Christ's ethic for men to-day. On the one hand, his teaching primarily concerns committed Christians. On the other hand, we must remember that we Christians to whom its

[2] *The Sermon on the Mount,* 15.
[3] *The Teaching of Jesus,* 294.
[4] *The Synoptic Gospels,* II, 27.

terrifying challenges come are not invited to rise to these heights in our own strength.

III

Our third thesis, that Jesus in his ethical teaching enunciated great principles in the manner of the prophets rather than laid down legally binding rules of conduct, has been well stated by B. W. Bacon. 'The Sermon is not legislative,' he says, 'but prophetic. It does not enact, but interprets. It does not lay down rules, but opens up principles.'[5] James Denney was making the same judgment when he wrote to Sir William Robertson Nicoll, 'It would be a great point gained if people would only consider that it was a Sermon, and was *preached*, not an *act* which was passed'.[6]

Yet all down the Christian centuries men have sought to find in the Sermon a new law with rules to be literally and legally enforced. In the opinion of B. W. Bacon and other scholars Matthew conceived Jesus as a new Moses giving the New Law on a new Sinai. By Cyprian's time the process of turning the Sermon into law was far advanced. At the time of the Reformation the Anabaptists took the same view. And almost in our own day we have had Tolstoy literalizing and wanting to legalize the Sermon.

The proof that it is not a new law is in the Sermon itself, as A. D. Lindsay[7] has shown:

'Human laws or codes are based on calculations of how most men may reasonably be expected to behave. It is assumed that with a reasonable amount of effort such rules will get themselves kept. A law that is not going to be kept, which asks of people more than they are most of them at all intending to give, is a bad law It would be of no use making a law or moral code in order to put pressure on

---

[5] *The Sermon on the Mount*, 109.
[6] *Letters to William Robertson Nicoll*, 71.
[7] *The Moral Teaching of Jesus*, 96f.

men and women to be saints. That the Sermon on the Mount does ask us to be exactly this, in itself shows that it cannot be regarded seriously and yet treated as legislation. For Jesus told men, not as a command but as a revelation and a hope, that men are to be perfect even as our Father in heaven is perfect.'

In other words, the teaching of Jesus in the Sermon simply does not begin to square with what we understand by law.

The same conclusion is reached if we approach the problem from the angle of Jesus' conflicts with the scribes and Pharisees and the religion of legalism generally. It is at bottom a conflict between the prophetic spirit and the legal. The scribe or legalist thinks that character is determined by conduct, and that what must be done is to frame a code of morals telling people how they must act in any particular case. So there arise the 613 precepts of the Pentateuch or the Mishnah's thirty-nine kinds of work forbidden on the Sabbath. Jesus' approach is quite different. He is concerned not with acts, but like the prophets, with persons and principles. He finds the secret of good living not in obedience to a multiplicity of rules and regulations—i.e. a moral standard and authority imposed from without—but in the spontaneous activity of a transformed character. And therefore, as T. W. Manson says, 'it is a mistake to regard the ethical teaching of Jesus as a New Law in the sense of a reformed and simplified exposition of the Old, or as a code of rules to take the place of the code of Moses and his successors'.[8]

But what about the imperatives in Matt. 5.21-48? A glance at even the first of these will show that we must not —we cannot—treat Jesus' imperative as a law to be enforced by any body of men whatsoever. 'But I say unto you, that everyone who is angry with his brother shall be in danger of the judgment.' A court can judge the overt act of

[8] *The Teaching of Jesus*, 301.

murder; but what court can begin to judge the angry passion in a man's heart? Only God can do that. The truth is that to regard Jesus as a second Moses and his Sermon as a new code of laws is to relapse into that soul-destroying legalism which he condemned. The manner of Jesus is not legal but prophetic. He is in the same spiritual line as the prophet who said, 'Let judgment run down as waters and righteousness as a mighty stream' (Amos 5.24), or that other who declared on the question of divorce: 'Let none deal treacherously against the wife of his youth. For I hate putting away, saith the Lord, the God of Israel' (Mal. 2.15f.). He does not traffic, as the legalist does, in rules and regulations to cover every conceivable act of conduct. He lays down deep and far-ranging principles. He enunciates the ideals and aims that ought to govern the lives of men who are living in that new order of grace which he calls the Kingdom of God. In short, the teaching of Jesus as we have it in the Sermon resembles 'a compass rather than an ordnance map; it gives direction rather than directions'.[9] It is a design, not a code, for life in the Kingdom.

I V

The ethic of Jesus is an unattainable ethic which we, as his followers, are nevertheless challenged to attain—this is our last thesis.

'All this Sermon on the Mount business,' says one of Rose Macaulay's characters, 'is most saddening. Because it's about impossibilities. You can receive a sacrament, and you can find salvation, but you can't live the Sermon on the Mount.'

This quotation poses the question, 'Can we *use* the Sermon on the Mount today, and if so, how?'

Before we can even dream of using it, we must (as we have tried to do) get at the real meaning of the Sermon.

[9] T. W. Manson, *The Sayings of Jesus*, 37.

This means making due allowance for figurative language, poetic form, Oriental hyperbole and paradox. It means also taking into consideration the men and the conditions to which its teaching was originally addressed. We must also remember that the Sermon does not give us a complete account of Jesus' teaching, and that many of the situations and problems—social, economic and political—which trouble us never came within his horizon.

These considerations, though they make the task of using the Sermon more difficult, do not entitle us as sincere Christians to dodge the issue, either by saying with the man of the world, 'You can't live the Sermon. It's about impossibilities', or with the Roman Catholic Church, 'This is not for the rank and file of Christians but for a certain few called to lead the religious life'. As we call ourselves followers of Christ, we must acknowledge that Christ does set before us a real design for living which challenges every thoughtful disciple. He does tell us: (1) the kind of people we ought to be; (2) the influence we ought to exert in the world; (3) the way in which, as Christians, we ought to behave socially; (4) the kind of worship we ought to render; (5) the attitude we ought to have towards earthly and heavenly treasures; and (6) the manner in which we should treat our fellow-men. And most of us know, as Dr Joad says, that 'Christ's prescription for good living . . . is the right prescription'.

'Relevant, then, in this sense,' a man may admit, 'but is it practicable?'

Here we must beware of two extreme views of answering the question.

Many Protestant scholars write as though Christ's purpose in the Sermon were simply to show us how utterly we fall short of the pure will of God set forth in his teaching, and so, through a sense of failure and despair, prepare us for the message of salvation in the Cross. In his able book *Christ's Strange Work* Dr A. R. Vidler called the Sermon 'a terrifying summons to repentance' and declared that it brings home to us 'our awful separation from the Saviour and our complete dependence upon him'.[10] This can be misleading. It is true that the Sermon, by showing us how God means men to live, convicts every earnest man of his sinfulness. In the pure and holy light of the Sermon 'all our righteousnesses are as filthy rags'. But we are surely right in doubting whether Christ *meant* the Sermon to be 'a terrifying summons to repentance', utterly 'unfulfillable', designed only to make us cast ourselves on the Saviour for forgiveness.

At the other end of the scale are those who blandly argue for the practicability of the Sermon. The view we have just mentioned they dismiss as an illegitimate theologizing (or 'Paulinizing') of the Sermon. They maintain that Jesus meant his precepts to be practised, and that they can be practised. Here, in our view, are both truth and error. We agree that our Lord did not mean his precepts to be mere counsels of perfection, utterly beyond man's power to fulfil. We appeal in proof to the parable of the Two Houses and to such a saying as, 'Why do you call me Lord, Lord, and do not the things which I say?' Nevertheless, we cannot accept the assumption that men can and do live according to the pattern shown them in the Sermon on the Mount. Here the argument from experience is final. No man—not even the best—keeps himself quite free from anger or hate or impure thoughts; none forgives without reservation; none trusts God with a faith unshadowed by any hint of anxiety; none loves without a limit. When Hans Windisch argued in his book for the 'fulfillability' of the Sermon, Rudolph Bultmann replied with an *ad hominem* question, 'Will Windisch claim that he fulfils the demands of the Sermon? Or does he assume that some other man does? Then why not?'[11]

[10] 1944 edition, p. 63.
[11] *Glauben und Verstehen*, 199.

Yet Jesus meant his ethic to be a real design for living, not a blue-print for Utopia. Further, we must never forget that the Sermon is an ethic for those who call Christ Lord and Saviour, for those who have entered the Kingdom of God and are promised the power and guidance of the Holy Spirit. (See the Epistle to the Romans. It is only after Paul has set forth the 'sin of man' [Rom. 1.17-3.20] and 'the grace of God' [3.20-8.39] that he sets before his readers 'the Christian ethic' [Rom. 12.1ff.].) In other words, we are not asked to scale the heights of the Sermon in our own un-aided strength: we are offered the continuing presence, through the Spirit, of him who promised, 'Lo, I am with you alway'.

In that assurance we can face the challenge of the Sermon, being always careful to avoid the temptations of legalizing its demands or trying to water them down. And beyond any question the Sermon can and does give us stimulus and guidance for the adventure of Christian living. Its standards ought to be before us when we make the personal decisions of Christian action. In any given moral dilemma, the Christian may ask himself, 'What light and help can I derive from the principles and precepts of my Lord, as I know them from the Sermon?' Having done this, he will be the better able to deal with specific moral choices. In the last resort, the way in which a man will respond to the demand of Jesus will depend on his own conscience (which the Sermon will greatly sensitize and sharpen), the guidance of the Spirit, and the shared wisdom of his fellow-Christians.

'Not as though I had already attained, either were already perfect.' Paul said that,[12] near the end of his life; and it is a great deal truer of us than of the apostle. Though the Sermon is our standard, it will always be beyond us. That is as it should be:

[12] Phil. 3.12.

> A man's reach should exceed his grasp,
> Or what's a heaven for?

No man, this side eternity, measures up to the Sermon's standard. We judge ourselves by it, and know that we are sinners. Yet if neither we, nor the first disciples, ever reached the heights to which Christ summons us, this is but an illustration of the tension between the ideal and the actual which must ever mark the life of Christ's disciples, now as then. For we have to live our lives at once as citizens of this world, with all its trials and temptations, and as citizens of the Kingdom of God.

'Christ's ethic,' it has been truly said,[13] 'stands for the unattainable which we are yet bound to attain.' Thus and thus, says Jesus in the Sermon, should his disciples live as citizens of the Kingdom. Though we, no more than the first disciples, can ever hope to reach the ideal in this fallen world, we are summoned day by day, with the help of the Spirit, to make the effort. For it is Design for Life in the Kingdom of God.

[13] W. Manson, *Jesus the Messiah*, 85.

INDEX OF SUBJECTS AND NAMES

Adultery, 51f.
Agape, 60f.
Almsgiving, 64f.
Anabaptists, 56, 116
Angaros, 59
Apecho, 65
Athanasius, 45
Augustine, 76

Bacon, B. W., 116
Battalogeo, 67
Beatitudes, 33ff., 115
Ben Sira, 36
Benedictions, the eighteen, 69
Bengel, 46, 87, 94
Bentham, 21, 113
Blake, 112
Bonhoeffer, 105f.
Brooks, 87
Bultmann, 120
Burney, 18f.
Burns, 39, 86
Buttrick, 38

Carlyle, 71
Catholicity, 29, 60, 62
Celsus, 24
Chesterton, 20
Comforter, 36
Confucius, 90
Cullmann, 38

Davies, 17
Dead Sea Scrolls, 35

Deane, 12
Debts, 76
Denney, 116
Devil, 56, 77f.
Devine, 34
Discrimination, 87f.
Divorce, 53ff.
Duncan, 'Rabbi', 51

Elbogen, 69
Epiousios, 75
Essenes, 55
Exceptive Clause, 54
Eye, the single, 81f.

Fasting, 78f.
Father, God as, 71f., 89
Fitzgerald, 20
Forgiveness, 75f., 78
Forsyth, 76
Frost, 103

Gandhi, 9, 99, 107
Gesinnungs-ethik, 101f.
Gore, 88, 91, 115
Grace, 15f., 35, 43, 104f.

Helikia, 85
Hell, 52, 92
Herrmann, 101f.
Hillel, 24, 26, 40, 53f., 87, 90
Holland, Scott, 109
Houses, parable of Two, 95f.

Inge, 112
Interims-ethik, 100f.

Jeremias, 43, 78, 104
Joad, 29, 119
Jot and tittle, 48
Judging, 86f.

Kaddish, 69, 72
Kant, 91
Kingdom of God, 16, 34f., 43, 72f., 114
Kittel, 28, 102

Lao Tsze, 24
Law, William, 59
Law and grace, 15f., 104f.
Lewis, C. S., 25, 42
Lillie, 47
Lindsay, 52, 62, 116
Lord's Prayer, 67ff., 115
Luther, 36, 94
Lynch, 74

Macaulay, Rose, 118
Maltby, 58
Manson, T. W., 47, 59, 115, 117
Manson, W., 122
Marshall, 28
'Matthew', 13
McArthur, 99
Meekness, 37
Mercy, 38
Merit, 39, 43
Moffatt, 23, 87
Money, use of, 80f.
Montefiore, 39, 41, 58, 61, 66, 115
Mourners, 36
Murder, 49f.

Nestlé, 75
Nicoll, Sir W. R., 108
Nietzsche, 9

Oaths, 55f.
Oglethorpe, 78
Origen, 22, 85
Orginality of Sermon, 24ff.

Parables, 20f., 43, 51
Parallelism, poetic, 18f.
Paul, 15f., 23, 40, 43, 45, 69, 103, 108, 121
Peacemakers, 40
Peirasmos, 77
Pentateuch, 15, 117
'Perfect', 62
Plain, Sermon on, 14
Plato, 24
Prayer, 65ff., 88ff.
Proverbs, 22f.

'Q', 13 *et passim*
Quakers, 55f.

Raca, 50
Retaliation, 56ff.
Reward, 41ff.
Rhythm, poetic, 19f.
Riesenfeld, 13
Righteousness, 37f., 40, 85
Rihbany, 56
Rule, the Golden, 29, 90f.

Salt and Light, 44f.
Sanday, 27
Schweitzer, 100f.
Scott, C. A., 42, 57
Seeing God, 39
Seneca, 24
Servant of the Lord, 35, 40f., 45, 59

Shakespeare, 25f.
Shammai, 53
'Splinter and Plank', 87
Swearing, 56

Talmud, 27
Taylor, A. E., 28
Temple, 39, 74
Tolstoy, 56, 86, 99f., 116
Torrey, 62
Tradition, 12f.
Treasures, 80f.
Trust, 82ff.

Vidler, 119f.
Vision, the Beatific, 34, 40, 43
Von Hügel, 60
Votaw, 26f.

Ways, the Two, 91f.
Weiss, J., 83f.
Wellhausen, 28
Wesley, J., 78
Wilder, 35
Wilson, Edward, 67, 84f.
Windisch, 120
Worship, 63f.

INDEX OF CHIEF SCRIPTURE
REFERENCES

OLD TESTAMENT

Genesis
2.23-24   53

Exodus
20.7   55
21.12   50
21.23-25   57

Leviticus
19.2   62
19.12   55
19.18   61
24.17   50
24.17-21   57

Deuteronomy
18.13   62
19.16-21   57
24.1   53

Psalms
6.9   95
19.1   18
24.3f.   39
37.11   37
39.5   85
41.1   64

Proverbs
10.1   18

Isaiah
49.6   45
51.1   38

Isaiah—cont.
51.6   59
52.7ff.   73
58.5   79
61.1   35

Amos
5.24   118

Micah
6.8   38

Malachi
2.15f.   118

APOCRYPHA

Tobit
4.15   90
12.8f.   64

Ecclus
48.24   36

NEW TESTAMENT

Matthew
5.1   11
5.3-12   33-41
5.13-16   44-46
5.17-20   46-48
5.21-26   49-51
5.27-30   51f.
5.31-32   53-55
5.33-37   55f.
5.38-42   56-59
5.43-48   60-63

Matthew—cont.

5.44f.	24
6.1-4	64f.
6.5-8	65-67
6.9-13	20, 67-78
6.14-15	78
6.16-18	78f
6.19-21	80f.
6.22-24	81f.
6.25-34	82-86
7.1-5	86f.
7.6	19, 21, 87f.
7.7-11	88-90
7.7f.	19
7.12	90f.
7.13f.	92
7.15-23	93-95
7.24-27	95f.
19.1-12	53
20.1-16	43
25.31-46	38, 43

Mark

1.15	73
4.21	45
10.2-12	53
10.45	92
11.25	78
12.29-31	91
15.21	59

Luke

2.25	36
6.31	90
6.36	38
6.47-49	95
10.30-37	61
11.2f.	67-78
11.9-13	88f.

Luke—cont.

11.33	45
11.39	39
12.15	80
12.22-31	83
12.58f.	51
13.23f.	92
16.17	47
16.18	53
16.19-31	38
17.7-10	43

Romans

8.14ff.	40

I Corinthians

4.9	45
7.10f.	53
9.27	23
15.3ff.	108

I Timothy

6.10	80

James

1.13	77
5.12	56

I Peter

1.4	37
3.14	40

I John

1.8	76

Revelation

7.17	36
22.4	40